THE RULES OF HAPPINESS

Pearson

At Pearson, we have a simple mission: to help people make more of their lives through learning.

We combine innovative learning technology with trusted content and educational expertise to provide engaging and effective learning experiences that serve people wherever and whenever they are learning.

From classroom to boardroom, our curriculum materials, digital learning tools and testing programmes help to educate millions of people worldwide – more than any other private enterprise.

Every day our work helps learning flourish, and wherever learning flourishes, so do people.

To learn more, please visit us at **www.pearson.com**

THE
RULES
OF
HAPPINESS

A personal code for finding your happiness

RICHARD TEMPLAR

Harlow, England • London • New York • Boston • San Francisco • Toronto • Sydney
Dubai • Singapore • Hong Kong • Tokyo • Seoul • Taipei • New Delhi
Cape Town • São Paulo • Mexico City • Madrid • Amsterdam • Munich • Paris • Milan

PEARSON EDUCATION LIMITED
KAO Two
KAO Park
Harlow CM17 9NA
United Kingdom
Tel: +44 (0)1279 623623
Web: www.pearson.com

First edition published 2026 (print and electronic)

© Richard Templar 2026 (print and electronic)

The right of Richard Templar to be identified as author of this work has been asserted by him in accordance with the Copyright, Designs and Patents Act 1988.

The print publication is protected by copyright. Prior to any prohibited reproduction, storage in a retrieval system, distribution or transmission in any form or by any means, electronic, mechanical, recording or otherwise, permission should be obtained from the publisher or, where applicable, a licence permitting restricted copying in the United Kingdom should be obtained from the Copyright Licensing Agency Ltd, Barnard's Inn, 86 Fetter Lane, London EC4A 1EN.

The ePublication is protected by copyright and must not be copied, reproduced, transferred, distributed, leased, licensed or publicly performed or used in any way except as specifically permitted in writing by the publishers, as allowed under the terms and conditions under which it was purchased, or as strictly permitted by applicable copyright law. Any unauthorised distribution or use of this text may be a direct infringement of the author's and the publisher's rights and those responsible may be liable in law accordingly.

All trademarks used herein are the property of their respective owners. The use of any trademark in this text does not vest in the author or publisher any trademark ownership rights in such trademarks, nor does the use of such trademarks imply any affiliation with or endorsement of this book by such owners.

Pearson Education is not responsible for the content of third-party internet sites.

ISBN: 978-1-292-47951-4 (print)
    978-1-292-74742-2 (ePub)

British Library Cataloguing-in-Publication Data
A catalogue record for the print edition is available from the British Library

Library of Congress Cataloging-in-Publication Data
A catalog record for the print edition is available from the Library of Congress

10 9 8 7 6 5 4 3 2 1
30 29 28 27 26

Cover design by Nick Redeyoff

Print edition typeset in 11/13, ITC Berkeley Oldstyle Pro by Straive
Printed in the UK by Bell and Bain Ltd, Glasgow

NOTE THAT ANY PAGE CROSS REFERENCES REFER TO THE PRINT EDITION

Contents

Acknowledgements xi
Introduction xiii
How to use the Rules xvii

Confidence 2

1 Find sure ground 4
2 Appreciate your value 6
3 Do what you're good at 8
4 Sidestep the negative 10
5 Take your time from A to Z 12
6 No comparison 14
7 Believe it 16
8 Just do it 18
9 Face it 20
10 Make your own decisions 22

Creativity 24

11 Get in the flow 26
12 Don't judge 28
13 Mess up 30
14 Achieve 32
15 Grapple 34
16 Be yourself 36

17 Collaborate 38
18 Get inspired 40
19 Change it up 42
20 Don't follow rules 44

Responsibility 46

21 Don't be a victim 48
22 Don't take on too much 50
23 Admit your mistakes 52
24 Take the blame 54
25 Your reactions are your own 56
26 Look after yourself 58
27 Look after other people 60
28 Welcome feedback 62
29 Be a good colleague 64
30 Have a social conscience 66

Giving 68

31 Giving comes in many forms 70
32 The more you give, the more you get 72
33 Let it drip 74
34 Choose your charities 76
35 Don't expect others to be indebted to you 78
36 Let people be themselves 80
37 Don't overdo it 82
38 Say thank you nicely 84

39 Be accepting 86
40 Let others give too 88

Mindfulness 90

41 Know your roots 92
42 Get the basics right 94
43 Breathe 96
44 Observe 98
45 It won't always work 100
46 Don't stop thinking 102
47 Stay detached 104
48 Open up 106
49 Retain your values 108
50 Feel your emotions 110

Time 112

51 Chores are necessary 114
52 Lean in 116
53 How you spend your day is how you spend your life 118
54 Strike the balance 120
55 Find your happy place 122
56 Don't get overstuffed 124
57 Prioritise regularly 126
58 Drop your standards 128
59 You control your phone 130
60 Be ready to jettison 132

Connection 134

61 Quality not quantity 136

62 Make the time count 138

63 Take it seriously 140

64 Take stock 142

65 Make it better 144

66 Change your angle 146

67 Talk to strangers 148

68 Get social 150

69 Make friends at work 152

70 Put down roots 154

Health 156

71 Get some sleep 158

72 Enjoy the fresh air 160

73 Get moving 162

74 Exercise more 164

75 Manage your energy 166

76 Eat well 168

77 Drink well 170

78 Don't poison yourself 172

79 Build your resistance 174

80 Think long term 176

Curiosity 178

81 The journey is more important than the destination 180
82 Ask yourself questions 182
83 Be inquisitive about people 184
84 Understand conflict 186
85 Take a deep dive 188
86 Look for adventure 190
87 Love a rabbit hole 192
88 Expand 194
89 Question your work 196
90 Reject boredom 198

Soul 200

91 Find a purpose 202
92 Live by your values 204
93 Find the awe 206
94 Have a ritual 208
95 Stop trying to find yourself 210
96 What goes around, comes around 212
97 Think about what comes next 214
98 Don't ask 'why me?' 216
99 Not all questions have answers 218
100 Get better and better 220

Create your own Rules 222

Index 223

Acknowledgements

With thanks to everyone who has helped me to be happy over the years. Special thanks to the people who have assisted with putting *The Rules of Happiness* together, in particular Mithago Craze and Elie Williams.

Introduction

It's impossible to write a book about happiness without questioning how to define it. If you look it up in a dictionary, you'll find it variously described as a state of feeling joy, delight, contentment, glee, pleasure, satisfaction, gladness, good mood. I don't know about you, but I think those are all different things. Some are fleeting while others are more lasting. Some hit a real high while others suggest more of a gentle buoyancy. So what is this book all about?

There are plenty of ways to get a momentary feeling of pleasure, delight, glee – most of them legal. Those emotions aren't hard to come by for most of us, even if they don't last. But once they've passed, you're back to your baseline. Your underlying mood, which might be low or high, good or bad, steady or erratic. And it's that baseline I'm interested in. That's about feelings that are more like contentment, or satisfaction.

If you have a baseline that is steady and contented, not only will you land back there after those brief highs, you'll also come back to it when you have lows. A bad day, or a stressful time at work, or a worrying family crisis is always going to get you down. However, if your underlying state is one where you're comfortable in your own skin, satisfied with your life in the broader sense, those inevitable gloomy moments won't last too long, and you'll be back to your usual, cheerful, flourishing self before long.

To be happy in this sense – to have an enduring feeling of optimism, cheerfulness, contentment – needs most areas of your life to be going well most of the time. It requires you to pay attention to the things that contribute to happiness, which aren't always the things that are shouting for your attention.

On the plus side, however, there's been no shortage of studies done into what it is that gives people this long-term, underlying happiness. Of course there isn't one simple, straightforward answer – eat more carrots, or hug a tree every day – or we'd all be doing it already. There are several things that go into the mix, and you need to pay attention to as many of them as you can.

Mind you, they aren't difficult. The challenge is to identify the ones that you most need to work on, and then to incorporate them into your life until they become a habit. And that's what *The Rules of Happiness* is all about. I'm here to help you recognise where you can improve your happiness levels, and give you some pointers to doing just that. I've divided the book into ten key areas that have been shown to have a positive impact. It's no coincidence that there's a link between curiosity and creativity, for instance, or between giving and connecting with people, so I've put each Rule into the section I think fits it best. Overall there are plenty of Rules to help you; and you don't have to start practising all of them at once. If you want lasting happiness, it's worth taking a little time to assemble the building blocks in order to give yourself a solid foundation.

The important thing to understand about happiness is that it doesn't lie in wealth or career success or material possessions. Study after study has shown that while there can be a short-term hit from achieving these things, people soon settle back to a point where they take them for granted, and the pleasure of having them abates. Psychologists call it the 'arrival fallacy' – the mistaken belief that once you arrive at a particular point in life that will make everything OK. You just need this job, or that qualification, or this income.

The problem with the arrival fallacy is that not only does it not work, it actively hampers you. It makes you live in the future, not valuing what you already have. That can lead you to ignore the people around you as you chase fame and glory, and then find your relationships have suffered for something that doesn't actually feel worth it. When attaining your goals doesn't bring you happiness, you can find yourself wondering what the point is, and perhaps even questioning whether you're doing something wrong.

It's understandable why people who lack material things would think that having them would make them happy, but the good news is that you can be perfectly happy without them. You only have to look around you. Are the richest, the most successful people always the happiest? Of course not. You can find miserable rich people the world over, and you can also find happy people living in poverty. If it was all about material goods, that wouldn't be possible.

How happy you are can certainly be influenced by your genes, your experiences, your circumstances, your personal relationships. But that ignores just how much of it is within your own control. This book is packed full of Rules you can follow that put you in charge of your own happiness. You might not score ten out of ten every day – that would be unrealistic – but you can make sure that your baseline maintains a good, healthy score.

None of the Rules in this book cost you money. Some of them may take a little time, or a change of habit, but they're all things that any of us can achieve if we're willing to focus on them. They will give you a sense of living a life that is worthwhile, and isn't dependent on external luck, or the vicissitudes of your career, or on anyone else. They will help you to be content with what you have, confident in what you believe in, and comfortable in your own skin. And we all deserve that.

Richard Templar

How to use the Rules

It can be a bit daunting to read a book with 100 Rules for a happier more successful life. I mean, where do you start? You'll probably find you follow a few of them already, but how can you be expected to learn dozens of new Rules all at once and start putting them all into practice? Don't panic, you don't have to. Remember, you don't have to do anything – you're doing this because you want to. Let's keep it at a manageable level so you go on wanting to.

You can go about this any way you like, but if you want advice, here's what I recommend. Go through the book and pick out three or four Rules that you feel would make a big difference to you, or that jumped out at you when you first read them, or that seem like a good starting point for you. Write them down here:

Just work on these for a couple of weeks until they've become ingrained and you don't have to try so hard with them. They've become a habit. Great stuff, well done. Now you can repeat the exercise with a few more Rules you'd like to tackle next. Write them here:

Excellent. Now you're really making progress. Keep working through the Rules at your own pace – there's no rush. Before long you'll find you're really getting on top of all the Rules that will help you, and more and more of them are becoming ingrained. And voilà! Congratulations – you're a proper Rules Player.

CONFIDENCE

You won't be surprised to know that there's a positive correlation between confidence and happiness. It's what you might expect, and indeed research shows that more confident people are also happier. Although confidence and self-esteem aren't the same thing, if you're more confident your self-esteem is likely to be greater too. So if you feel comfortable in your own skin, you feel safe, you believe in your abilities, you're secure, why wouldn't you feel happy?

Happiness isn't about money, success, power. We all know people who manage to be happy without any of these things. Nevertheless, although money can't buy you happiness, it can buy you out of a lot of unhappiness. And one of the benefits of building your confidence is that, actually, you'll be better placed for financial and career success. Confident people sell themselves well, they're persuasive, they can make decisions more easily, they stand up for themselves, they can take risks more readily, put themselves forward, focus on their strengths, stretch themselves, cope with setbacks, learn readily from mistakes.

That's an impressive list of benefits from increasing your confidence, and obviously they will help you beyond just your career. Those skills will help your relationships too. Of course some people seem to be born confident and others – through nature or nurture – find it comes less naturally. Nevertheless, if you follow the next few Rules, you can increase in confidence. And the best news is, it's self-perpetuating. The more confident you become, the easier it is to build these Rules into your life.

RULE 1

Find sure ground

Even if you think your confidence is really low compared to most people you know, we all have some areas where we can be sure of ourselves. You might feel uncomfortable in social situations, but know you're good at your job. Or maybe you're less sure about work, but confident you're a good listener. Perhaps you recognise that you're hugely knowledgeable about butterflies, or your local football team, or Roman history. Or you've created a beautiful garden (even if you don't feel brave enough to show it to people), or you're certain your family absolutely know how much you love them.

I know someone who gets very anxious socially, and would describe himself as under-confident. When forced into social situations he copes well and is extremely well-liked, but he can't see it. On the other hand, he's massively knowledgeable about antique jewellery, and can talk at length about it with complete assurance. That's one thing he *is* confident about.

There'll be something for you too. Probably several things, however large or small, and however under-confident you feel in other areas. You'll probably notice, too, that you have many of the skills that come with confidence in those areas. For example, my antique jewellery expert is very comfortable making decisions about what jewellery to invest in, and if he makes a mistake he learns from it, without it denting his underlying confidence.

You might feel you're under-assertive around other people, unwilling to put yourself forward, reluctant to attempt anything new around them. However, that may not be the case with your own family. If you have kids you might be perfectly assertive when necessary, and happy to take the lead. If that's the case, you clearly have those skills. Sure, you might find them easier to access with some people than others, but you should draw strength – confidence indeed – from the fact that you can do this.

You simply need to broaden the circumstances where you trust yourself to show this side of yourself.

Look, everyone has strengths. So make sure you know what yours are. If you don't like to blow your own trumpet, you don't have to tell anyone else.* But think about the areas you do actually know you're solid in, or even shine. There – that's what confidence feels like. You just need to help it leak into other areas of your life too.

> **THERE – THAT'S WHAT CONFIDENCE FEELS LIKE**

---

* Maybe modesty is one of them?

RULE 2

Appreciate your value

Who do you spend more time with than anyone else? Yep, yourself. Twenty-four hours a day. And it's pretty hard to feel confident in yourself if you don't like what you see. Not to mention the fact that if you have to hang out with someone seven days a week, it's much more pleasant if you enjoy their company. Now listen – it is within everyone's power to be likeable. There are more than enough factors that are under your control, so it isn't possible for you not to be a likeable person if you want to be, even if for some reason you don't believe it at the moment.

By the way, just because you're likeable, it doesn't mean you can't sometimes be irritating. I don't know anyone who can't occasionally be irritating. Maybe I'm just grumpy, but most of the people I love have the odd trait or habit that niggles. I still love them though. And goodness knows I irritate myself endlessly.* People are never perfect, and that goes for you and me along with the rest of them. Doesn't matter. It doesn't make us worth less, or harder to like. In fact if you did manage to be perfect, you'd be pretty unbearable. So still not perfect then.

This is about perception. That's all. You are likeable, and the only question is whether or not you can see it. You might love yourself, hate yourself, think you're sort of OK, like yourself on a good day. If you're not a big fan, that might be your natural starting point, or it might be the result of your past experiences. Trauma, especially in childhood, can be hugely damaging and I'm not about to address it in a few hundred words here. But if your view of yourself is less than positive, please recognise that it's about your perception – it's not reality – and it's worth getting help to redress it if you can't do it alone.

I've talked about why confidence is so important to your happiness across all areas your life, and you won't achieve all the confidence

---

* Why can I never remember to drink my tea before it goes cold?

you could unless you learn to like yourself. How can you possibly express your views firmly, be assertive, make strong decisions, be persuasive, play to your strengths, if you don't believe you have value? That you're worth paying attention to?

So what is it that makes people likeable? Essentially it's about having strong, positive values and doing your best to follow them. No one lives up to their own standards all the time, but if you're genuinely trying to be kind, fair, honest, considerate, you'll be as likeable as the next person. You need to know what those values are – some will be shared with pretty much all likeable people, and others might be more personal, such as being eco-friendly, or pacifist. Think about people who you like, or don't particularly care for, and analyse what it is that makes them so.

As well as striving to follow your own values, the other thing that contributes to likeability is allowing others to be themselves. We don't generally care for being told what to do or how to think or behave. So absolutely discuss your views with other people, but don't try to control people's thoughts or behaviour. That takes a bit more effort for some people than for others, but it's the effort that counts, even if you sometimes look back and feel you could have played that conversation or scenario a bit differently. We all do that. What matters is that you care.

> **IT ISN'T POSSIBLE FOR YOU NOT TO BE A LIKEABLE PERSON IF YOU WANT TO BE**

RULE 3

Do what you're good at

This might sound obvious but actually, there are reasons why we don't always do what we're good at. Maybe we don't enjoy it, or we enjoy something else more, or we don't like doing what other people tell us to. This often starts at school or uni when we pick the subjects our parents or teachers are suggesting, or we don't choose the subjects we excel at because we don't like the teacher. Maybe you really want to be a doctor and make subject choices accordingly, even though your flair is for History or French.

It can happen in adulthood as well, of course, when we take the job that pays most, or gives us the commute or holiday entitlement we prefer. We've been star of the local basketball team but we give it up when we have kids. And look, that's all fine. There are lots of reasons for taking this job or that, and for spending your free time any way you choose.

But right now, we're talking about confidence. If you're brimming with the stuff, that's fine.* However, if you're less confident than you'd like – and more confidence would make you happier – it's worth factoring it into this kind of decision. We've already established that everyone feels confident in some part of their life, and you just have to recognise your areas of expertise, from handling your tricky mother to being able to recite pi to 25 decimal places, or whatever. Now imagine being able to have that confidence in your work or your social life, and make the choices that will help you.

If being good at basketball boosts your confidence, maybe give up something different when your time is limited, or at least cut it down instead of stopping completely. If you're applying for a new job, take into account the importance of doing something you know you're good at. Even if the pay's not quite so good, or

---

* And you've probably skipped this whole section (note to self – so who am I saying this to?)

the hours are a bit longer, the knock-on effects on your confidence and happiness might still make it worthwhile. It can still stretch you of course – if you're confident in that field you'll be happy to be stretched.

When you're choosing subjects for study – at school or uni or evening class – think very hard about where your skills really are. That's where you'll gain the most confidence, when you know you can get good results and learn the most. And that confidence will spread through the rest of your life too. It will make you feel you're a capable person, and that has to be good for you. No, no, I'm not saying you *have* to do that subject if you don't want to – come on, have the confidence to tell me where to get off if you like. I'm saying you should acknowledge that picking Sport when you're way better at Chemistry, or car maintenance when you have a real knack for electronics, is not going to help your confidence. Factor it into the equation and then make your own decision.

If you're serious about becoming more confident, and thereby happier and better equipped to cope with life, it matters that you make choices which maximise your opportunities to feel capable and competent. The more time you spend in that frame of mind, the more readily you'll slip into it naturally, and the better you'll develop the skills that go with it and which you can apply elsewhere.

> **IT WILL MAKE YOU FEEL YOU'RE A CAPABLE PERSON, AND THAT HAS TO BE GOOD FOR YOU**

RULE 4

Sidestep the negative

It would be lovely if all your confidence came from the inside, and you could cope with any kind of knocks and setbacks without it being dented. That's rare though, very rare. We're a social species, and inevitably we're affected by the feedback we get from other people, spoken or unspoken, diplomatic or tactless.

Some of that feedback is genuinely helpful, and expressed in a supportive and encouraging way that makes you feel you're learning. Good feedback should build your confidence by acknowledging your strengths and giving you the chance to build on them.

Not always the way though, is it? Some people always seem to look for the negative, to criticise, to put you down. The reasons they do it are their stuff, but it has an impact on you. It's easy to find yourself losing confidence and seeing only the negative. You can begin to doubt your ability in whatever area they're highlighting – your work, your dress sense, your singing, your tennis serve, your writing style.

And sometimes – which is worse – you begin to doubt your value as a person. A combination of their criticism and your reduced self-esteem can leave you feeling it's *you* that's not good enough, not just your work or your cooking or your choice of shoes. Like I say, this is actually about their need to bring you down, even if it's not intended on their part. It should always be possible to give feedback only when asked, and then in a constructive way. But this is real life, and you won't be lucky enough only to encounter people who are positive.

You need to be hanging out with people who give you a positive boost, so some of these negative people are best avoided. But of course some of them are good friends in other ways, and don't intend to deflate you. They simply don't understand the effect they have. If you're looking to build your confidence, like most of us, you want to sidestep their feedback. Certainly don't ask for it, and don't put yourself in line for it either – don't ask them round for a meal you've cooked yourself, for example, or give them tickets for your next amateur musical show. Don't tell yourself they're more honest than other people and you need to hear their reaction. You don't need to hear it, being negative is not the same as being honest, and anyway who says they're right?

Of course there's another group of people who are harder to survive unscathed. These are the people who too often give unsolicited negative opinions, and can't be avoided – your boss, your parents, your close family. You can be slowly ground down over years by your boss's constant criticism, or your mother's endless carping. This is never easy, but keep reminding yourself it's about them, not you. Doubtless they do it with other people too. If it becomes too big a problem, you might need to put space between you – start looking for another job, or visit your parents less often. Don't share information with family that you don't need to if it's bound to attract criticism.

You can also prepare for it, ideally with a co-conspirator. Tell yourself in advance that it's guaranteed to happen, and see if you can guess what they'll pick this time to berate you with. Then report back afterwards and see how accurate you were, and what their pickiest criticism was, or their most passive-aggressive remark. This turns it into a kind of game, and gives you a distance that can help you to stay detached.

> **IT'S ABOUT THEM, NOT YOU**

RULE 5

Take your time from A to Z

How old are you now – and how long has your confidence been a bit fragile for? Very possibly all of that time, right back from early childhood. Maybe it's a broad sense of self-doubt, or perhaps it's just in certain areas of your life. It will be a combination of nature and nurture, and you may or may not be able to untangle all the causes of it. Wherever it comes from, it's hampering you from reaching your full potential, and that gets in the way of your happiness.

Well, now you can start to get to grips with it. The Rules in this section will give you a solid foundation for building yourself up. Take them one at a time, or in groups – whatever works for you – and resolve to build up your self-assurance in whatever areas you feel the need. You don't need to become the world's most confident person. You just want to feel comfortable doing the things that used to be tricky, to the point where lack of confidence isn't getting in your way.

Most of us become more confident as we get older, unless we're very unlucky and take major hits to our psyche. That's partly because we get better at sticking to our comfort zone, and partly because the more you do anything, the more confident you become in your ability to do it again. Of course, it can be a good thing to move out of your comfort zone, and that's where building your confidence helps you find the courage to try something new. A self-assured cook is much more likely to brave a tricky recipe than one who isn't certain they can get beyond toast or boiled eggs.

That's how the process in these Rules works. You edge ever further out of your present comfort zone, making sure of your footing before going a little bit further. There will be the occasional leap, but mostly it's a steady, step-by-step thing. Just like growing more confident with age, only this time it will progress with more pace because it's conscious and deliberate.

Don't be unrealistic though. You won't turn into a new person overnight, and don't doubt yourself when that doesn't happen. This is about small steps – but they all add up. I don't want your confidence to suffer when there's no magic wand, or all your good work will be wasted.

So expect progress, but also expect it to take time. Notice all those little incremental improvements and give yourself a pat on the back. 'I didn't stumble once during that presentation', or 'My mum criticised my clothes and I genuinely didn't care', or 'I was brave enough to cook a meal for friends and it went fine'. These are important, not just because the meal was good, but because you were confident enough to cook it.

Not only do you need to recognise the positives, you also need to acknowledge that there will be the odd hiccup. It doesn't mean the whole thing is falling apart. It's normal. Even top chefs produce the odd dish they feel didn't go as well as they'd have liked. This is just normal. It's the big picture trajectory that matters, and never mind the occasional glitch. Two steps forward, one step back is still progress, eh? Don't set yourself deadlines or targets. Just take it easy, focus on the small gains, and when you look up, there'll be a real difference.

> **THIS IS ABOUT SMALL STEPS – BUT THEY ALL ADD UP**

RULE 6

No comparison

In almost any walk of life, there'll always be someone who is 'better' than you. More skilled, more experienced, more accomplished. And there'll be someone who's better than them too. There are eight billion people on the planet, after all. What's more, in any creative sphere, it's a subjective judgement. Who is the better artist, musician, chef, actor, architect, designer? Not everyone will even agree.

You can always find someone to compare yourself with unfavourably. That doesn't prove anything. Confident people don't do that. They might notice when they're better than someone else (although if they're Rules Players they won't gloat). It's just a fact. Here's someone who's had a bit more practice at this, or someone with less of a flair for that. It doesn't have anything to say about them, it's merely an observation.

Confident people know they're still a beginner at this, they're getting pretty good at that, they've always had an eye for this, they could be really good at that with a bit more practice. If you want to be more confident, the first step is to stop comparing yourself with other people. You know what you want to achieve, so just work towards it at your own pace, and celebrate those steps forward.

Here's another thing confident people (like you're going to be) are good at. They know their own abilities and they don't really mind what you think, or what anyone else thinks. They don't need your validation. Yes, of course there's a warm feeling when someone you respect notices and comments favourably. But if you're secure in your own abilities, other people's opinions won't change it. If you're a really good home cook, and you know it, it won't matter if some fancy Cordon Bleu typè looks down their nose at your food. You're not trying to please them, and you're happy with the kind of dishes you want to serve up.

Of course this is all easy to say, harder to do, but once you understand this, you can catch yourself fretting about other people's opinions and realise that they don't matter. You can train yourself to look at others who maybe work faster than you, or earn more, or whose home-baked bread turns out perfect every time, and simply recognise that they've had a bit more experience, or practice, or luck. Doesn't matter what. If your bread is perfect most of the time, or only occasionally but your hit rate is improving,* then you're doing what you set out to.

As always, find the areas where this works for you, and remind yourself how it feels. The things you noted in Rule 1 that you are confident about. Your ability as a parent, your project management skills, your knowledge of antique jewellery, your DIY. You don't compare yourself unfavourably with other people there, and you don't need someone else to tell you you've put that shelf up straight, because you know it already.

> **YOU DON'T NEED SOMEONE ELSE TO TELL YOU YOU'VE PUT THAT SHELF UP STRAIGHT, BECAUSE YOU KNOW IT ALREADY**

---

* There's a joke in there somewhere about proving bread, but I can't be bothered

RULE 7

Believe it

Why are we so inclined to doubt ourselves? We take up a new sport or hobby, or start a new job or relationship, and then we spend our time worrying we're making a hash of it. I know a woman who got a great job, which involved four weeks' training before taking control of her own project. She spent the whole month feeling literally sick with worry that she couldn't do it, so anxious that she barely took in anything the trainer was saying, and therefore even more convinced she'd fail as soon as she was left on her own. She was a nervous wreck, hardly sleeping, and unable to socialise with her new colleagues because she felt so inadequate.

At the end of the month, the training came to an end and she was expected to get on with the job. And guess what? It turned out to be so well within her capabilities that she really didn't need the training that she hadn't been able to listen to anyway. She'd been miserable for a month simply because she didn't believe in her ability to do the job.

The thing is, she only applied for the job because it was a really good fit for her capabilities. The company weren't idiots, and they gave her the job because they could see she'd be good at it. And yet all of that was eclipsed by her own lack of self-belief. Of course, her confidence will be that little bit stronger another time after that experience, and after a couple of years of being successful in the job.

Many of us are capable of just the same lack of belief, which damages our confidence, and in this case made her really unhappy for several weeks. And yet . . . why would you apply for a job you didn't think you could do? Why take up a sport you're bound to be rubbish at, or start a hobby you have no propensity for, or go into a relationship you can't possibly make work? Deep down, some part of you must believe, or you wouldn't have got yourself into this position. The problem is that once you're committed, you start to doubt yourself.

Listen to your inner monologue. What are you telling yourself? Don't allow yourself to go down the 'what if I can't do it?' route. Don't try to dredge up examples of mistakes you've made in the past that prove things will go wrong. Instead, tell yourself 'they wouldn't have offered me the job if they didn't believe I could do it', or 'I'm a decent football player, so of course I can learn hockey', or 'I've never had my own pet before, but I grew up with cats so I'm not learning from scratch'.*

No one is looking for perfection from the start. Whether it's a new job, a new baby, a new skill, of course there will be mistakes. That's how learning works. Suppose you're learning to drive. That can be pretty nerve-wracking to begin with. But why did you start unless you believe you can learn? And if everyone else can learn it, why wouldn't you be able to? There are two options here – believe in yourself, or don't. So why not pick the one that works? The one that helps you to feel confident?

> **LISTEN TO YOUR INNER MONOLOGUE. WHAT ARE YOU TELLING YOURSELF?**

---

* You're welcome

RULE 8

Just do it

Sometimes you feel unsure of yourself and teeter on the edge. Shall I sign up for this class? Shall I apply for this job? Should I book this great holiday, even if it means travelling by plane? You're not confident you can cope, so you hesitate to even start. Goodness knows that's understandable, but there are a lot of reasons to ignore your doubts and jump in with both feet.

For one thing, many of these scary propositions will carry you along in the flow if you just take the first step. If you apply for the job and get an interview, you'll be swept along because it's harder to back out further downstream. On the other hand, you're not committed, so at that early stage you can tell yourself – quite genuinely – that you don't have to attend an interview if you get one, or take the job if it's offered. So right at the start is the easiest place to grab the opportunity. If you don't, there won't be another chance to opt in or out.

I started a whole business that way. I wasn't sure about it, but I just took the first step. When that went well, I took the next one, and within a few months I had a company up and running. Turned out to be much less scary than I thought. Hard work, lots to learn, but perfectly possible.

Once you've done the easy bit – filling out the form or clicking the button or making the booking – you've set things in train to get the thing done. Learn a new skill, go on a great holiday, move on in your career. And that's important, not only because you want those things, but because it shows you that you can do it. Behave as if you were confident, and next time you will be that bit more confident because you've done it before. You've learnt that you're capable of applying for a new job, or travelling by air, so each time it gets easier.

Maybe the challenge is more immediate. Your boss asks if you'd be up for giving part of a presentation, or your local committee ask you to stand for election as chair. My Rule has always been to say yes to these things, especially if they seem daunting. Once you've said yes, you're committed, so then you'll have to do it. Which means you'll get the chance to prove to yourself that you can. You'll have a brief flurry of 'what have I done?' followed by the deep satisfaction of doing the thing, and then the long-term confidence of knowing that you can because you've done it before.

Other people have done these things successfully before, so why can't you? Remember to believe in yourself – your boss, or your committee members, clearly do. And then prepare and practise and rehearse and plan, whatever is applicable, so you absolutely know it will go well. That's what everyone else does. And the more you've gone over and over it, the more confident you'll feel. There'll still be a few butterflies on the day, of course – that's because you care. It doesn't mean you can't do it. In fact, it means you're more likely to do a great job because you're taking it seriously. And maybe the butterflies are also giving away a little bit of excitement about realising that you're the kind of person who *can* do this.

> **YOU'LL BE SWEPT ALONG BECAUSE IT'S HARDER TO BACK OUT FURTHER DOWNSTREAM**

RULE 9

Face it

I know several people who are terrified of spiders, as I'm sure you do. You may even be one of them. Or if it's not spiders it could be birds, moths, flying, public speaking, loud noises. Several of the people I know who feel this way do everything they can to avoid spiders. They check their bedroom for spiders every night, or they don't visit places or countries that are known for their flourishing spider populations. There are friends they won't stay with because they live in old, spidery houses, and they check their shoes for critters every morning before they put them on.

I have some sympathy here of course, but there's an inherent problem with this approach. It starts right from when they tell you they're scared of spiders. Our subconscious mind hears everything, and every time you tell someone else you're scared, you're reinforcing it in your own mind. Not only that, but every time you check the room for spiders, you're telling yourself it's essential that there are no spiders here. And some of these people can't visit certain friends, or travel to certain places, because of their fears.

This kind of anxiety is a huge lack of confidence in a specific area. You might be otherwise low in confidence, or you might be the most confident person imaginable in other parts of your life. Either way, when it comes to spiders, flying or whatever it is, you've lost all confidence in your own ability to cope. And you've done that to the extent that it really interferes with your life.

I used to know a woman who was so scared of birds that she couldn't shop in her local town unless one of her kids was with her, giving a constant running commentary of 'there's a pigeon ahead to your left but, don't worry, it's standing still', or 'there's a blackbird on the tree over there – it's OK I'm keeping an eye on it'. She was perfectly confident in other ways, but the fact that her kids had been recruited to help in this way reinforced her own belief that she couldn't even nip out for a pint of milk on her own.

Over time these fears can go from feeling anxious to being really restrictive, and controlling your actions. We're thinking about your happiness here, and how happy can you be if you have no confidence in coping with this kind of fear? If you were terrified of some kind of scenario you're never likely to encounter – going into space, or being forced to eat sheep's eyes – it probably won't matter. But it's just no good going through life unable to cope with spiders, or train travel, or giving a presentation.

The only recourse – if you want to get your confidence back – is to learn to cope with these things. You don't have to love them, just tolerate them. Stop reinforcing your own fear. Stop telling yourself (and other people) that you're 'terrified' and start saying you're 'not a fan' or you 'don't much like' them. Stop consciously searching the room or checking your shoes. And then actively seek out ways to reduce your fear to a manageable level. Hacks, strategies, therapies, whatever it takes. I know several people who have gone from 'hating' spiders to being able to pick them up with a glass and a piece of card. They don't want to keep them as pets, or actually touch them, but what matters is that they really never think about spiders anymore unless they see one. At which point they just deal with it.

> **YOU DON'T HAVE TO LOVE THEM, JUST TOLERATE THEM**

RULE 10

Make your own decisions

Confidence comes in many forms, and we've looked at several of them now. Irrational fears can be very restrictive, and make it hard to relax and feel chilled and happy, as the last Rule showed. And now here's a very different manifestation of low confidence, which also needs addressing if you want to be more self-assured.

One of my friends is forever asking her partner for advice. If she's clearing out her wardrobe she'll ask, 'Do you think I need this coat?'. She works freelance from home, and will ask him, 'Do you reckon it's OK to take this morning off?'. When it's her turn to cook, she'll double check with him before deciding what to make. She has no confidence in her ability to run her own life, so she continually seeks reassurance.

What most forms of low confidence have in common is that they tend to be self-perpetuating. Every time you ask someone else's opinion, or check your shoes for spiders, or decide not to apply for that new job, you reinforce your own view that you can't do the thing. If you get into the habit of checking your decisions with others before committing yourself, you stop trusting yourself to make the next decision or the one after.

Some people (like my friend) do this generally, and for some it's more specific. For example, you might feel insecure about your ability as a parent and check all your decisions with your mum, but be sure of yourself at work. Maybe you're on solid ground in your own home, but need lots of reassurance before any social event – Is it OK to wear this? Will I be able to help myself to a drink? What if I'm tired and want to leave early?

Sometimes seeking reassurance can sound a lot like asking advice. Lots of people ask their mum or dad for parenting advice, and not all of them lack confidence. The difference is in how you feel. Do you think you know how to deal with this, but would find a second opinion or a different perspective helpful? Or do you worry that you'll get it wrong if you don't get help with the decision? Are you happy managing this part of your life alone, but other people's input is useful? Or are you anxious that things will go wrong, and need to double-check with someone else to be sure it's OK? If the latter is the case, your confidence could do with boosting in order that you can feel happy about making your own choices when there's no one around to ask.

It takes practice, as always, but you can start now. Do the easiest bits first – stop asking someone else where to put the cutlery away and work it out for yourself. If you're offered a hot drink, don't ask questions – Shall I? What are you having? – just answer, 'Thank you. Tea would be lovely.' These are small things, but you're sending yourself an important message, and getting into the right habits.

Then learn the principles of social engagements, or parenting, or whatever it is, so you have the knowledge to make your own decisions. Look, you probably already know them, but it's the same principle as give someone a fish and feed them for a day, teach them to fish and you feed them for life. Teach yourself how to pick a wardrobe, or raise kids, and then stop asking for help. Start making the smaller decisions yourself, and build up until you're only ever asking for a second opinion. You'll feel so much more relaxed, and confident of your ability to run your own life.

> **WHAT MOST FORMS OF LOW CONFIDENCE HAVE IN COMMON IS THAT THEY TEND TO BE SELF-PERPETUATING**

CREATIVITY

One of the things that can add considerably to your happiness is being creative in some way. Research shows that not only does having this outlet make you feel happy and relaxed, it can also reduce depression and anxiety, and even pain. Specific forms of creative expression have their own benefits too. For example dance improves mobility and balance, gardening can reduce blood pressure, creative writing can boost your mood, and so on.

It's worth making time to be creative – or making more time than you already do. Everyone is capable of being creative in some way from performing to cooking, writing to home decorating, fashion to photography. You can improve at all of these activities the more you do them, although it's not about being accomplished or winning prizes.

And don't forget that one of the most creative things you can do is problem solving, which is an invaluable skill at work as well as at home. Together with the related ability to generate ideas, this is a strength which will really help your career. A lot of it is about thinking freely, without constraint, and that's a habit that all forms of creativity will help you develop.

The more varied your creative outlets, the more benefit you'll get from them. It's great to spend all your free time painting watercolours, but even better if you can find some space also to garden or write poetry or make music. Each of these will exercise different parts of your creative brain, so don't be afraid to look for new outlets even if you are already creative. These Rules should help you to exploit the artistic and innovative side of yourself fully, so you can maximise the enjoyment you get from it.

RULE 11

Get in the flow

One of the great benefits of almost all creative pursuits is that they enable you to get into a state of deep focus and enjoyment, often known as flow.* You might also think of it as being in the zone. It's that state where you're so engrossed in what you're doing that you lose sight of everything else. That means you forget your worries and cares, your ego, your sense of time. Some argue that this is the closest to happiness that you can get.

If you're serious about exercising the creative side of yourself, this is what you're aiming for. Of course there will be times you only have five minutes to spare, or you're doodling while you're on the phone, or thinking as you drive. But aim to set up the right conditions for flow when you can, because that will give you the most benefit.

Those conditions will vary according to what you're doing, so you'll need to think them through for yourself. For example, you want to allow yourself enough time to get into the activity fully – how much that is will depend on what you're doing. And you'll want to minimise the chance of interruptions that will break your flow. You might want solitude, but you can be very creative alongside other people too, so that will depend on what you're doing and how you're doing it.

Some people find their surroundings really matter to them. Perhaps they need to be outside, or they want the right music in the background, or they need to be in their own workshop or study or studio. Mind you, changing this up occasionally might be stimulating in a positive way.

Another important factor for achieving flow is making sure that you set yourself a task or a challenge that is neither too easy nor too difficult. That should be a pretty broad window, mind you.

---

* A term coined by psychologist Mihaly Csikszentmihalyi if you're interested

However you can't really get into the zone if there's no challenge to the task, nor if it's simply too difficult. You need to feel up to the exercise you've set yourself, but only if you're properly focused. There's the sweet spot you're after.

When it all comes together, you lose yourself in the task entirely, in the sense that you forget about yourself, your own ego, and can see only the challenge in front of you. Your mind is entirely in the present, fixed firmly on what you're doing, oblivious to everything else. That's as calm and inspiring as it gets.

> **YOU FORGET YOUR WORRIES AND CARES, YOUR EGO, YOUR SENSE OF TIME**

RULE 12

Don't judge

The whole point about being creative is that you're free to explore ideas and techniques and possibilities. You may have a starting point, but the end point is open to you. Even when you're using your creative skills to solve problems, there will be parameters but so long as you keep within them, the solution might be anything.

The fastest way to shut down this open and free expression is to pass judgement on it. To make you feel that your painting isn't good enough, your taste is poor, your skills aren't up to scratch, your cooking doesn't inspire. It makes you feel that you should stop even trying, and it's antithetical to the creative approach.

So don't look at what you've created and conclude that it's bad or wrong. That's not a thing in the creative world. Of course there are times when what you produce isn't a good match for some purpose you want to put it to – displaying it in an exhibition, entering it for a competition, serving it up to guests – but that doesn't make it bad in itself. The object of the exercise is to lose yourself, to open your mind, to explore. If you've done that, how can it be bad?

Try to get into the habit of looking only for the positive, if you must form an opinion. Find a turn of phrase you're pleased with, or the way a shadow falls, or a particular move, or a combination of fabrics that works. Not because you need to mark the thing out of ten, but because it might spark an idea for next time.

If you're used to engaging in brainstorming sessions at work, you'll know – if they've been well run – that one of the ground rules is that there should be no judgement. If someone makes a suggestion you don't think will work, you keep it to yourself. There will be opportunities later to question it, if it even gets taken forward. Brainstorming at its best is a highly creative exercise, and the participants have to feel free to throw out all ideas, however shaky they might be, in case they can be developed, or they spark someone else to come up with something productive. If people are worried their suggestions will be jumped on or criticised, they'll clam up. And that's the enemy of creative thinking.

So don't shut yourself down, and avoid people who will negatively criticise your creations. Any photography or creative writing society, or performance group, or cookery or gardening club that passes judgement on what you do isn't helpful. Constructive criticism, absolutely – if you ask for feedback – but it must be positive. Similarly, any work-based problem solving or brainstorming groups that don't adhere firmly to the 'no judgement' rule are not going to be a fraction as productive as they could be.

> **THE OBJECT OF THE EXERCISE IS TO LOSE YOURSELF, TO OPEN YOUR MIND, TO EXPLORE. IF YOU'VE DONE THAT, HOW CAN IT BE BAD?**

RULE 13

Mess up

So, no judgement. And that makes this next Rule much easier to follow. If nobody – yourself included – is judging what you do, then you can do anything. What could be more creative? You can experiment, mess around, scribble, put things together weirdly, whatever you like. And that's actively a good thing.

Everyone knows that mistakes are supposed to be a good thing, they're how we learn, if you never made a mistake you'd never make anything blah, blah. We all know it, but apparently we don't really believe it, or we wouldn't mind so much when we get things wrong. When we're at school, why do teachers mark us down when we make mistakes, if it's such a good thing? Why do our parents give us a hard time when we mess up as teenagers? When we're at work, why does the boss complain if we get something wrong?

It *should* be true that mistakes are a positive learning tool – assuming we were trying our best – but life too often teaches us that even if we learn from them, we still have to be punished or reprimanded or sanctioned for them.

But finally, here in your creative world, where no one is standing by with a red pen to mark you, you really can make all the mistakes you like. Deliberately, unintentionally, it's all fine. And that's if you can even tell it's a 'mistake' because who's to say what's right and what's wrong? Right and wrong have no meaning here.

Sometimes you might want to paint a picture that actually looks like the subject, or write a poem that scans, or build a table that doesn't wobble. Or you might not. Maybe you wanted it to wobble. But so many creative judgements are entirely subjective anyway. If you think these cushions look great with this paint colour, then as far as you're concerned, they do. If someone else disagrees it doesn't make your view any more right or wrong.

If you try to 'get it right' you constrain yourself, and leave yourself open to failure, if only in your own eyes. So don't aim for that. Just do what you like and see what happens, then build on the bits you like and maybe decide not to go down certain routes again for a while, or not in the same way. It doesn't mean you can never enjoy the satisfaction of a painting where you've just caught the sense you wanted, or a table that doesn't wobble, or a poem that scans, or a performance that moves someone to tears or laughter. But really throw yourself into the joy of doing the thing for its own sake, in the way that a small child relishes play-dough, or dressing-up, or splashing paint around, without worrying about what the end result will be. See if you can't regain that childish joy in creating for its own sake.

> **RIGHT AND WRONG HAVE NO MEANING HERE**

RULE 14

Achieve

Following on from the last Rule, and just to add a bit of nuance, it is OK to complete something and feel good about it. While it can hamper the creative spirit always to be aiming for that, it's no bad thing to give yourself the occasional target.

Theatre, dance and film-making are all examples of highly creative pursuits where the aim is frequently to produce a final piece for other people's enjoyment. The start of the process might be very experimental and improvised, but there comes a point where you bring the threads together and work towards a particular date or finished piece.

This isn't compulsory, and all forms of art can be practised on your own, with no time limit or end point, if you like it that way. However sometimes the constraints of a deadline or an audience can help the creative juices. You might continue to tinker afterwards – as a playwright might re-edit the script next time around – or you might feel that now you've completed your painting, or composed your piece of music, you're happy with it as it is and ready to move on.

Look, obviously there's nothing wrong with saying 'I've finished, and it's complete'. You only have to look at da Vinci, or Austen, or Beethoven, to see that they produced finished pieces of work. They might have wanted to go back and fine-tune, I wouldn't know, but at some point they stopped and said 'It's done'.

Of course some things can never really be finished. A garden won't stop growing and changing just because you've got it how you want it. In a sense the same goes for making your house look the way you like. You might cook the perfect meal, but as we all know, you can't have your meal and eat it. You can record a performance, but you can't recreate the experience of watching it live. Nevertheless, there's the sense of an end point, even if it isn't permanent.

One of the upsides of completing a creative project is that it gives you a feeling of accomplishment. The fact you've finished the novel or completed the picture or given the performance creates a sense of achievement. And the feeling that we've achieved something is really good for our self-esteem, and makes a significant contribution to our levels of happiness.

So find the balance that works for you, between freeform expression which might take you anywhere, and working towards an end goal. Both of these have an important part to play, and it will help you enormously if you understand what they both do for you, and how you can find the best of both worlds.

> **THE FEELING THAT WE'VE ACHIEVED SOMETHING IS REALLY GOOD FOR OUR SELF-ESTEEM**

RULE 15

Grapple

As I mentioned before, problem solving can be hugely creative, and if you're trying to solve a conundrum relating to something you really enjoy, it's not hard to get in the flow. It might be a dilemma at work, or it could be related to your other creative outlets – for example it might be the logistics of designing a piece of furniture, or how to get a particular effect in a performance, or how to light a photograph so the shadows work but the subject is still recognisable.

Some problems can be solved easily, but others can take days of turning them over in your mind until you find a solution that really sings. And boy, is it satisfying when that happens – not to mention boosting your self-esteem and making you feel happy. You need to look at the problem from all sides, and from no side, if you're going to find an answer where there isn't an obvious one. There are lots of techniques and ways of approaching this kind of exercise,* but the key is not to go down the traditional route, whatever that might be. If you want to be creative and innovative, you need to find a new angle.

Question everything. Don't assume anything, just because you've done it that way before, or that's what everyone says you should do. Try removing elements you thought were essential, or starting from a step further back. For example, when he invented the modern sewing machine, Elias Howe cracked the problem when he put the eye at the pointed end of the needle. That was the opposite of where it had been for millennia on a hand-sewing needle. It takes a really creative mind not to accept that as a given but to think 'what if . . .'.

Often problems are created by certain parameters – you need to operate to this timeframe, or this budget, or within this structure, or using these resources. Of course these should be one of the

---

* Some of the Rules for this are outlined in *The Rules of Thinking*

first things you question when the problem is knotty – what if we didn't have to do it this way? Maybe those parameters don't have to be as fixed as you first thought, or maybe working out what you'd do if money was no object will spark an idea you can adapt to fit your budget.

However these constraints can be a positive. One friend, who designed their own house, told me that every time the builders said 'We can't do this' or 'That product has been discontinued' or 'This is way out of budget', they had to go back to the drawing board. And every single time they came up with a solution that was actually better than the original plan. Without the constraints – in other words built as planned – the house would have been less satisfactory. That's a great example of how satisfying and productive parameters can be when you're solving problems creatively.

> **YOU NEED TO LOOK AT THE PROBLEM FROM ALL SIDES, AND FROM NO SIDE**

RULE 16

Be yourself

In a sense all forms of creativity are self-expression, because being creative is about being original – rather than just painting-by-numbers – so the only possible source of that creative expression is yourself. Nevertheless, some works of art (in the broadest sense) will be more personal than others.

The more you can be yourself – express yourself – when you're being creative, the more it can help you with your mental health. If that's not why you're doing it, that's obviously fine, although it's always good for your confidence and your sense of self to put your own thoughts and feelings into what you do. If you're using a creative outlet actively to help boost your self-esteem, or deal with difficult emotions, the more of yourself you put into it, the more cathartic it can be.

When I first started out as a writer, I wrote in a pretty neutral style. It wasn't about me – and I wasn't writing fiction – so I focused on putting across the most useful ideas in a logical order, using a style that was easy to read, and written in the third person. Nowadays, being more confident and less worried about what publishers might think, I write as myself. Hello – this is me here. I'm writing in the first person, and including personal examples – like this one.*

Imagine being a professional interior designer. Your job is to be creative, but your client will insist on a budget, and they hate pink, and they won't get rid of that ugly sofa, and they want lots of swags at the window even though you've tried to suggest a plainer treatment would work best. So you take those parameters – which we've seen can be very stimulating – and you come up with a lovely creative design. However, it won't be nearly as personal as your own living room at home, where you've done exactly as you please.

---

* And the occasional meta observation, like this

Both of these approaches – both living rooms – can be wonderful and creative. But it's the one in your own home that will be the most self-expressive, and therefore have the most positive benefits for your psyche. That's the one that will communicate the most about who you really are, and will strengthen your sense of self-identity, and your confidence in being yourself. And that confidence and sense of identity will add to your happiness.

These options exist whether you're performing, painting, gardening, taking photos, cooking, decorating your living room, or being creative in any other way. If you can not only be yourself but also use your creativity to express troubling emotions, that can be a great therapy.

You might know that the seventeenth century poet John Donne is a favourite of mine. He wrote about his feelings partly because, as he put it, 'Grief brought to numbers cannot be so fierce, For he tames it, that fetters it in verse.'

> **THE MORE OF YOURSELF YOU PUT INTO IT, THE MORE CATHARTIC IT CAN BE**

RULE 17

Collaborate

If you're going to be creative, why do it alone? The more people, the more ideas – and often you can spark off each other and come up with creations that are so much more than the sum of their parts. That's not an end in itself for our purposes – we're all about how being creative can make you happier – but a really successful project can be a part of that, as we saw a couple of Rules back.

Look, this isn't compulsory, and it doesn't work for everyone. However many of us derive huge pleasure from being part of a team, from a sense of belonging, and that can extend into our creative lives too. Ask any successful theatre company or dance group. The feeling when you're all pulling in the same direction, that sense of coming together in unison, can be uplifting and invigorating.

Maybe your chosen outlet is writing, and you don't fancy joining a writers' group. That's fine, but you can have more than one creative outlet. Maybe keep writing alone but join a choir. Cook alone but take up painting lessons. Work with your partner to give the garden a makeover.

If you're producing ideas or projects in a group, sometimes people will disagree with you. If that's done in the right way – and you listen and accept it – it can be a really positive and productive process. Your idea isn't necessarily right or wrong, but that process of give and take, listening and being respectful, giving everyone a chance, adds to the sense of being part of a team.

This is something that you often encounter at work – depending on your job – where you all put your heads together to come up with ideas and improvements, or to design a product or an event, or to solve a tricky problem. At its best, it leads to innovative outcomes that you all feel you've contributed to, but no one can really remember who came up with which bits because it was such a team effort.

Of course I realise that isn't always how it feels. Sometimes it's hard work in the wrong way, and leaves you feeling sapped and drained – quite possibly without ever arriving at a good solution. If this is happening at work, you have to find a way to deal with it, and hopefully you will. However, if this is some creative pursuit you're following because it makes you feel good, there's not much point if it's making you miserable or frustrated. Obviously you'll see if there's some way to resolve it, or to put up with it, but in the end it's OK to walk away if it's not doing anything for you. Maybe find a different group, with different personalities, or another creative outlet you can share with other people.

It's not 'giving up' if you want to do that. Remember why you're doing this – to feel more fulfilled and to stimulate your creative juices. If that's not happening, you're not obliged to keep flogging a dead horse. It's your choice, so do whatever makes you feel best.

THAT SENSE OF COMING TOGETHER IN UNISON CAN BE UPLIFTING AND INVIGORATING

RULE 18

Get inspired

If you're serious about being creative, you'll find that the more creative you are, the more opportunity there is for self-expression. You can find inspiration in all kinds of places, to spark you into producing something new and different. Especially if you actively look for it.

I know a gardener who visited Derek Jarman's famous garden on the south coast of England. Jarman's house was on a huge shingle bank which is populated by wild plants, and littered with flotsam and driftwood. He created an extraordinary garden that was simply an extension of this, a greater concentration of those natural plants, interspersed with driftwood and sculptural finds from the beach. Without fences, it's hard to see where the garden ends and the natural landscape begins.

My gardener acquaintance was inspired by this, but doesn't live on a shingle bank. So he started to incorporate into his own country garden some of these same principles, encouraging plants that were similar to those in the surrounding fields that formed their backdrop. It's a completely different garden to Jarman's, but it only exists because of the inspiration his garden gave them.

Lots of gardeners will tell you how visiting other gardens gives inspiration, whether it's a theme for a flower bed, or a particular combination of plants. Great cooks are similarly inspired by dishes they've eaten, and ingredients they've discovered. This follows no matter what your personal outlet, from painting to dancing, filmmaking to sculpture. What's more, the stimulus can cross disciplines, so a poster that catches your eye might inspire your home makeover, or a beautiful piece of music might trigger you to produce an original painting. Feeling inspired actually triggers a release of dopamine – often known as the 'feel-good hormone' – which helps you to learn, and to feel motivated.

The moral of this is that the more you seek out inspiration, of all kinds, the more creative you'll become. So get out in nature, travel if you have the opportunity, read books, visit galleries and museums, go to theatre and music shows. You don't have to do all of these – this isn't an order – but if you want to be more innovative and original in your creations, and free to express yourself as openly as you can, the more the better. Consciously think about why you enjoy this, or find that moving, or indeed dislike something, because that will help you find your own inspiration.

Many people also find it helpful to collect scrapbooks of quotes or images or ephemera – either physically or online – to look through. These can give you a jumping off point for a new project or work of art, and give you inspiration if ever you're feeling out of ideas. Just because the original spark might come from elsewhere, it doesn't make your creation any less personal and original. Indeed that might be the thing that makes it truly inspiring to someone else.

> **THE MORE YOU SEEK OUT INSPIRATION, OF ALL KINDS, THE MORE CREATIVE YOU'LL BECOME**

RULE 19

Change it up

Different creative activities stimulate different parts of your brain. If you've ever looked after small children all day, or worked on a production line, you'll know that sense of frustration and stagnation when you only exercise one small part of your brain. If your life is usually more stimulating than that you might be less aware of the dormant parts of your mind, but it's still the case that some of it isn't getting the exercise it might.

It follows that this is true of our creative brains specifically, as much as the larger picture. Within your brain as a whole it's healthy to exercise the creative element. And within the creative part, it's good to flex all your metaphorical muscles – to fire on all neurological cylinders.

Once you've started to make more time to be creative, and are seeing the benefits in terms of the relaxation and enjoyment it brings, you want to start looking for ways to extend what you're doing into new challenges that make you think deeper or in new ways. Think about this – the point of being creative is to use your brain in new and expressive ways. But if you keep doing the same thing over and over, there's nothing new or expressive about that. My grandfather used to paint. He only ever painted one thing though: the same red rose, with a drop of dew on its petals. I never really understood why he did it – I don't remember asking him – and now I question whether you could even call that creative, despite the fact that painting is generally seen as a creative activity.

So make sure you don't get stuck in a rut. If you paint, not only could you paint something that isn't a rose, maybe you could try landscapes instead of still life, or acrylics instead of watercolour. If you cook, see what you could produce on a camp fire that's more than just sausages, or get into Indonesian or Spanish cookery. Try black & white photography for a change, or portraits – anything you haven't done before.

Another way to keep the originality flowing is to create a bigger challenge for yourself. Design a more complex piece of engineering, upgrade from a balcony garden to an allotment, write a whole novel instead of short stories. Stretch yourself further, and your brain will have to exercise itself more. And think how much more you'll get in the flow, and how much more satisfying the results will be.

You don't have to stick with the same discipline at all either. You can find a whole new way to excite your brain. You could extend your interest in fashion into interior furnishings, or expand from photography into film, or writing poetry into writing plays. Or hey, why not jump instead of stepping sideways. Just go straight from cookery to painting, or acting to dressmaking. You'd be surprised how many similarities you'll find between seemingly different activities, as well as stimulating differences.

> **THE POINT OF BEING CREATIVE IS TO USE YOUR BRAIN IN NEW AND EXPRESSIVE WAYS**

RULE 20

Don't follow rules

I'm a fine one to talk. Mr Rules here. But seriously, when you're being creative, the more rules you can break the better. That's when you start thinking for yourself, and that's always creative. You're looking for the opposite of painting-by-numbers, and that's painting-without-rules.

When you first start learning anything, from chemistry to drawing, you start with the basics. You learn the rules. When you cook, you start by cooking off the onions, then you add the liquid . . . for photography you line up the photo before you hit the button . . . in gardening you put the shorter plants at the front of the border and the taller ones at the back. Some of these rules are practical (if you don't make a watercolour paint wet, you can't apply it to the paper) and some are creative ground rules (don't wear brown and blue together).

That's fine to begin with, and it's very stimulating to paint your first rose even if you're following all the rules religiously. You're still being creative in a way you never have before. As time goes on, you start painting peonies too. Or snowdrops. Then you move on to landscapes, or acrylics. In the end though, however much you broaden your range, you're still limiting yourself if you only operate within these rules.

The fact is, some of these rules make more sense than others. A lot of them have exceptions, but you won't find out what they are if you never break them. Some of them are out of date. Some of them are valid if you're trying to produce a typical piece of art, but what if you're not? There's a rule that says if you're putting on a play, you should learn your lines before the opening night. Usually that's sound advice, but if you follow it blindly, how can you ever stage an improv show?

Look back at famous creatives and most of them are famous precisely because they broke the rules. One reason Shakespeare is still relevant today is because he ignored centuries of writing characters who were black and white, goodies or baddies, and created real people with the complexity of Hamlet or Lear. The impressionist painters were groundbreaking because they broke away from the accepted norm of painting realistic images in a studio, and instead worked outdoors to create pieces that didn't pretend to be indistinguishable from the real thing.

You may not aspire to be Shakespeare or Monet, but you can see how questioning the received wisdom, looking for alternative approaches, finding new ways to solve old problems, can be the very thing that unlocks the creative floodgates. Sometimes you'll find there's a good reason for this or that particular rule, and other times you'll discover that you can bend it or even break it to innovative effect. And you'll never know which until you try.

> **THAT'S WHEN YOU START THINKING FOR YOURSELF, AND THAT'S ALWAYS CREATIVE**

RESPONSIBILITY

The word 'responsibility' literally just means being able to respond. In other words, having control over how you react to the people and the world around you. That has its pros and its cons, of course. Let's acknowledge the downsides first – it means you can't blame anyone or anything else for the things that go wrong for you, because you're in charge of your own life. You also have to accept the consequences of your actions or decisions, even when they affect other people negatively.

On the positive side, however, it means you're free to do what works for you, unbound by other people's expectations or attitudes. Your life is your own, and you can choose the personal code you work to – being a Rules Player you will set yourself high standards, but you'll be in charge of living up to them.

And why will you do this? Well, being responsible isn't always easy but, because it puts you in control of your own life, it also puts you in control of your own happiness. It opens up possibilities and helps you become more confident and resilient, because you have some control over what will happen. It strengthens your relationships, both personally and at work. It can give you a sense of purpose, because once you're in charge you can make decisions about the things that matter to you.

The next group of Rules will show you how you can become more responsible at home, at work, and in the wider world. And by doing so, how you can take charge of your own happiness and success.

RULE 21

Don't be a victim

When you don't take responsibility for your life, the result is that you become, in effect, a victim – of fate, of other people's expectations, of circumstance. If you're not in charge, that's inevitable. Maybe you just get your head down and get on with it, or perhaps you become a martyr and complain about it.* Yes, it saves you having to think for yourself, or make decisions, but it's no fun.

In the end, if you're not as happy as you could be – and that's why we're here – you have to do something about it. If you don't like your job, or your relationship, or your living arrangements, or your work/life balance, then it's up to you to take responsibility and do something about it.

We all know people who spend their time bemoaning the fact that their boss expects them to stay late at work, or their partner never helps round the house, or the school PTA takes up too much of their time, or the kids never go to bed when they're told to. But all of these things are within their power either to change, or to walk away from. It might be scary or difficult, which is why playing the victim seems easier, but if they just took responsibility they could make it all OK. Talk to their boss or their partner, give up the PTA, be firmer with the kids. Or, of course, make a deliberate choice not to do any of those things – but then don't complain about it.

So don't let this be you. If you catch yourself complaining about your life, that's a sign you need to take responsibility and do something about it. Of course we all have a bit of a moan sometimes about the traffic, or the rubbish WiFi, or the weather. But don't complain about the things you could change, even if you don't want to change them, because then you're playing the victim.

---

* Which is what modern, everyday martyrs do. Real martyrs don't whinge, they quietly and stoically bear whatever life throws at them

But look, don't forget – if you're responsible for your life, you can take the credit for it too. When things go well, it's down to you. It was you who decided to jack in the job and start a business, you who got out of an unhappy relationship, you who cleared the time to go on holiday, you who took the leap and joined an art class, you who started going for a daily run.

However good your life is, that's credit to you if you've accepted responsibility for it. My wife was affronted a while back because a friend told her she was lucky to be married to someone who shared responsibility equally for the kids, the housework, and everything else. 'What do you mean, lucky?', replied my wife. 'I would never have married someone who didn't.' She wasn't going to let anyone get away with attributing to luck something she had made a deliberate choice over.*

So as well as creating the life you actually want, taking responsibility also allows you to take credit for your achievements. It might not be as easy as playing the victim, but it's infinitely more rewarding.

> **IF YOU CATCH YOURSELF COMPLAINING ABOUT YOUR LIFE, THAT'S A SIGN YOU NEED TO TAKE RESPONSIBILITY**

---

* Don't ask me why I picked that particular example to illustrate my point. If it paints me in a good light that's just luck

RULE 22

Don't take on too much

Right, so you're responsible for your own life, your choices, your decisions, your dreams, your happiness. And that's true for everyone else too. They are responsible for their lives, their choices, their dreams. Not your responsibility. So don't overload yourself with commitments you didn't deliberately sign up for, just because someone else thinks you should – or you *think* they think you should.

If we're all responsible for our own happiness, it can't be down to you if someone else isn't as happy as they might be. If they make a decision that affects you without clearing it with you first, that's their choice. You don't have to accept it. Suppose your boss promises a client something that requires you to work over the weekend. Remember – don't be a victim. Either make a deliberate choice to go along with it, or politely but firmly tell your boss it won't be possible. That may have consequences, and you'll be responsible for how you deal with them. But your boss's promises are their problem.

Other people's expectations – your boss or anyone else – are not your responsibility. Do your grown-up kids expect you to look after your grandchildren when they're at work? Does your partner assume you'll do all the driving when you're out together? Do the basketball club expect that you'll be free if they schedule an extra evening's training? Does your colleague just expect you to cover for them when they're late back from lunch?

None of these things is down to you, and you don't have to do them. Of course, you might be happy to, and that's fine. If you're not happy about it, you need to say so. It should be your decision, not theirs, and if you're responsible for your own life, you'll recognise that reality and take charge of deciding whether or not to do them.

And before you interrupt . . . no, I'm not saying you can let people down, leave them in the lurch. You're a Rules Player so that's not how you're going to handle this. If you've made a commitment, you'll honour it. Obviously. And you'll accept responsibility for making that undertaking even if you're now regretting it. But in future, you won't fall in with other people's expectations or plans without thinking it through for yourself and arriving at your own decision.

If you realise you're not happy with a long-term arrangement, you can give people fair warning that you're no longer going to be able to commit to it. Tell your partner or your boss or your colleague that the current set-up isn't working, and you need to discuss how to make things better. You need to recognise that you got yourself into this situation. Nevertheless don't let them fob you off – that's victim behaviour. Take responsibility for sorting things out one way or another from now on, without you being exploited.

> **OTHER PEOPLE'S EXPECTATIONS ARE NOT YOUR RESPONSIBILITY**

… RULE 23

Admit your mistakes

This is one of the more demanding aspects of being a responsible person. It is necessary however if you want the benefit of being in control of your own life, and you can't consider yourself responsible – in the best sense – until you can do this.

If this is all a bit new to you, and responsibility feels like a big ask, you can start by simply admitting your mistakes to yourself. No more blaming things on other people or on bad luck. Not everything is your fault, but be ready to admit to yourself honestly when you could have done things differently, made a different decision, reacted in some other way.

Suppose the traffic is terrible and you're late to work. It's made you so stressed that you can't focus and as a result you mess up the figures, or don't complete the day's work, or forget to call back a customer. Whose fault is that? Nope, not the traffic. Try again. Look, traffic always has the potential to be bad – if it matters that much you should have allowed extra time. Even so, the traffic isn't your fault, granted. But some people arrive late to work and then crack on and catch up by the end of the day, and do the job as well as if they'd arrived early. So whose fault is it that you haven't done that?

There's a nice Buddhist analogy that's relevant here, that says when something bad happens, two arrows head our way. The first delivers the pain of the misfortune, while the second is the pain we inflict on ourselves as a result. The second arrow is optional, if only we can see that it's in our power to avert it.

You've allowed yourself to get stressed, and allowed that to affect your work. Of course you didn't mean to, and you didn't cause the traffic jam (at least, I'm assuming you didn't). Nevertheless, you alone are responsible for how you responded to arriving late. That's the thing you have to admit to yourself. It's not easy to come to work calm when you've had a frustrating journey – it's entirely understandable that you found it hard to cope. But that doesn't mean you aren't still responsible.

And here's the important bit . . . you'll never arrive late to work and take it in your stride until you recognise that it's down to you to make that happen. You won't change anything if you think it's out of your control, because you'll believe you can't. Only when you acknowledge that you've made a mistake will you be able to do something about it. Leave earlier, learn to handle the stress differently or, better still, learn not to feel stressed when you're unavoidably late.

Whether a thing is entirely down to your mistake, or whether you've simply played a part in compounding someone else's mistake – or a piece of bad luck – there's no way you can learn until you recognise your part in it. You'll go on being a victim of bad traffic, or whatever else, forever. In other words, you'll never learn from your mistakes until you learn to recognise them as such.

> **YOU WON'T CHANGE ANYTHING IF YOU THINK IT'S OUT OF YOUR CONTROL, BECAUSE YOU'LL BELIEVE YOU CAN'T**

RULE 24

Take the blame

Once you've mastered the last Rule, you can graduate to this one. You're really getting the hang of this responsibility thing now. Once you've learnt to admit to yourself that you've made a mistake, it's time to learn how to say it out loud in front of other people. You don't have to own up to every tiny misjudgement or poor decision as if you were in some kind of confessional. You just have to take responsibility when other people are affected by your decisions, your actions, your mood, your attitude.

This can be really tough. There's a tendency to feel that by taking the blame we're drawing everyone's attention to how imperfect we are, that they'll think less of us once we've pointed out our own shortcomings.

There's a disconnect thing here though. You feel that if you admit your mistakes openly, and take the blame, that people will think worse of you. And yet . . . what do you think when you see someone else do it? Do you think worse of them? No, usually we admire people who have the honesty and integrity to admit they've messed up. We probably knew it anyway, and the people we might think less of are the ones who refuse to accept the blame even when everyone can see they're at fault. So which of those people would you actually like to be?

We respect people who take responsibility for their actions as reliable, and often courageous. We trust them. We know no one is perfect, and at least these people admit to being human. And because they own up openly to their mistakes, they can do what they need in order to put things right. On top of that, they show empathy and understanding by acknowledging the knock-on effect on us.

Gosh, doesn't that sound like just the kind of person you'd like to be? And you can. All you have to do is recognise where you've messed up, and say so out loud when it has an adverse effect on someone else. Simple. OK, it doesn't always feel simple. It's not easy if you're not used to doing it. But once you start, it gets easier. Practise by taking the blame for minor mistakes, or with the people you feel safest with. And remember, you're also accepting that you have control of your own actions, and that's good.

One last thing. If you've messed up, you have to accept responsibility properly. It's no good saying 'I forgot to call the customer back, but only because she gave me the message when I was busy doing something else.' Perhaps she did, and perhaps she shouldn't have, but that's irrelevant. You're taking the blame for the bit you're responsible for – forgetting to call the customer back. Full stop. If you try to take only partial blame, you're taking only partial responsibility for the mistake that *you* made. So just focus on your bit. Other people will join the dots for themselves if you weren't the only one responsible.

WE RESPECT PEOPLE WHO TAKE RESPONSIBILITY FOR THEIR ACTIONS AS RELIABLE, AND OFTEN COURAGEOUS

RULE 25

Your reactions are your own

We've touched on this already. When you embrace responsibility, you're accepting that you have control over your actions *and* your reactions. You're in charge, and that means being in charge of all your behaviour. You can't pick and choose which bits are your lookout and which you can abdicate from. It's a job lot.

You can't control other people, but you can control your reaction to them. Once you accept that no one can *make* you feel anything, that puts you in charge of your emotions, and gives you the power to respond in a way that works for you, not just a knee-jerk.

It sounds scary – it is scary – but it's also liberating. Yes, it means you have to do something about the feelings and behaviours you don't want to have; however it also means that you *can* do something about them. You aren't at the whim of how other people treat you. You can rise above it. Think how that will impact on your happiness, when you can choose which feelings you experience.

It's not easy. If it was easy, you'd be doing it already. For some of us it can be a lifetime of learning. You're progressing constantly though, so even if you never completely master certain feelings and reactions, you can still feel more in control day by day.

I've always been prone to stress – just ask my family. Very easily frustrated by day-to-day irritations, from rude customer service personnel to printers that refuse to print. Any little thing would get my hackles up – and that's before you consider the bigger upsets that come along every few days or so. And then I had a realisation, a lightbulb moment, when someone told me that all I had to do was choose not to be stressed. For just a moment, I wanted to hit them . . . and then I thought about it. I thought how wonderful it would be not to get ratty and frustrated twenty times a day. Imagine running late and not feeling my blood pressure rise. Suppose the printer broke and I just fixed it, or managed some other way.

Now, I almost never get stressed. I've accepted responsibility for that reaction – I'm not responsible for the customer service person, or the printer, but I can choose how I respond. I can have a broken printer and be stressed, or I can have a broken printer and not be stressed. Of course the occasional serious emotional worry still really gets to me, but the day-to-day stuff? That's a thing of the past. I may not have achieved perfection, but I'm massively happier than I was. I didn't enjoy being stressed, so now I hardly ever do it.

See, it is possible. But only once you recognise that you're in charge. Some reactions are learned over decades and reinforced by trauma or long experience, but hey, any improvement is worth having, and you'll make real progress in some areas even if others take longer. The important thing is knowing that, however hard it is, you're in the driving seat now.

> **NO ONE CAN *MAKE* YOU FEEL ANYTHING**

RULE 26

Look after yourself

The logical place to begin being responsible is with yourself. Your physical and emotional health, and your immediate environment. You're reading this book so you've already made a start, and recognised that your happiness is down to you. So you can start with the bits of you that are holding you back. Are you as fit and healthy as you'd like to be? Do you struggle with certain emotions or anxieties? Are you surrounded by clutter or washing-up? We'll look at some of those areas later on in more detail.* At this stage, the important thing is to acknowledge that if you're not happy, only you can fix it.

If you don't understand this, you'll make excuses – 'I'd like to be fitter but I don't have time to exercise', or 'I never get enough sleep because I have to be up so early', or 'My flat's so cluttered because there just isn't enough storage space', or 'I can't go on holiday abroad because I'm terrified of flying'. Yep, dumping all the responsibility on a lack of time, or space, or whatever.

But who's in charge of your time, your space, your mental health, if not you? Remember, taking responsibility means giving yourself choices. You're *choosing* how you spend your time, so if it doesn't allow you to exercise, or to sleep, that's your *choice*. Let's take the clutter as an example. It's very possible that all the stuff you own can't be stored neatly in your flat. But you could own less – there are people in this world who own no more than they can carry, and would be grateful to have your problem. It's perfectly possible to have a clear-out. Or maybe you could create more storage – put up some shelves or buy a cupboard. Or you could look for somewhere to live with better storage.

All these things are within your control. You don't have to do any of them if you don't want to. You can carry on stepping over piles of

---

* Incidentally, *The Rules of Success* is all about how to do exactly that – how to take control over all the important areas of your life

books and shoving things back into overflowing cupboards if you like. But you need to acknowledge that it's a choice you're making, and no one else – and nothing else – has inflicted it on you.

This isn't about beating yourself up over the mess, or over your lack of sleep or fitness or how unhealthily you eat. And of course not all the choices you have are easy ones. However, your own health and happiness and immediate environment are under your control, and at least you have choices once you recognise that.

> WHO'S IN CHARGE OF YOUR TIME, YOUR SPACE, YOUR MENTAL HEALTH, IF NOT YOU?

RULE 27

Look after other people

The last Rule was about being responsible for yourself. Now let's move on to other people. Hang on, haven't we established that you're not responsible for them? Well yes, we have – but you are responsible for how you interact with them. Human interaction is a two-way thing, and you're very much responsible for your end of it.

We've all witnessed or been involved in breakdowns of communication. Just recently a friend asked my advice on how much of something to buy, and I unthinkingly said 10 kilos instead of 1 kilo. They didn't question it, and then spent ten times as much money as necessary. Stupid of me. We all do it occasionally, and that's life, but we have to be prepared to hold our hands up to it. It's no good saying I was only trying to help, or they could have checked. Maybe, but that doesn't change my mistake.

Sometimes other people need context, even if they don't realise it, and you have to be one step ahead and tell them everything they need to know, not just the specifics. One of my close friends is hopeless at this, and recently told her partner she'd be working late. When she came home – half an hour late – she was deeply disappointed to find there was no food for her. Her partner had assumed she'd be much later so hadn't catered for her. She was annoyed, but in fact she was responsible for not being more specific – 'I'll be staying an extra half hour at work' would have been helpful, and avoided the problem. Yes, of course her partner might have asked the question, but it's my friend who had the necessary information, and has to take responsibility for passing it on. Or for the consequences when she fails to.

We also have a responsibility – especially we Rules Players – to do our best to be positive and encouraging to other people, and not to say or do things that will cause unnecessary upset. In other words, to do as we would be done by. Sometimes we have to broach a tricky topic, or break bad news, and we have to decide how to do that – or even whether to do it. We don't always get it right, but even when a mistake is honest and unintentional, we still have to be grown up and accept that we misjudged things. Otherwise how will we learn for next time?

Suppose one of your team members at work tells you their colleague is winding them up because they keep interrupting them. You dither about whether to speak to the colleague, unsure how to address it tactfully, and next thing you know they have a huge row. Of course you didn't know that was imminent, but you chose to delay talking to the colleague and you have to recognise your part in the consequences of that. Admit the mistake, accept the blame – not for their behaviour, but for letting things drift – and learn from it.

> **HUMAN INTERACTION IS A TWO-WAY THING, AND YOU'RE VERY MUCH RESPONSIBLE FOR YOUR END OF IT**

RULE 28

Welcome feedback

Hearing someone else criticise you, however constructively, can be tough. Well, I say that, but actually that's not generally what's happening. The problem is that it can feel like criticism is personal, a reflection on who you are. But constructive criticism is never aimed at you – it's aimed at your behaviour, your actions, your decisions.

If your self-esteem is low, it can be hard to hear any kind of feedback. That's because it's hard to separate your actions from your personality. So acknowledging any shortcoming feels like saying you're less of a person – that your choices and behaviours are a reflection on your innate character. That makes it no surprise at all that you don't want to hear someone tell you that your product launch could have gone more smoothly, or there were better ways to handle your sister-in-law, or your home-baked bread was a little bit stodgy. You're hearing that you're a rubbish organiser, your people skills are non-existent, and you can't cook.

But that's not what they said, is it? We all make mistakes, and actually there's no point giving feedback to someone who isn't capable of improving. What's happened here is that you've done a decent job, and there are useful things you can learn so it goes even better next time. When someone criticises you supportively, they're telling you that you have the capability to learn and develop, which is as much as anyone needs to do. Even the highest achievers want constructive feedback so they can achieve even more – top athletes, performers, artists.

Feedback is a good thing, and if you're able to listen openly and take it on board, you will get better at launching new products, handling tricky people, baking, or whatever it is. And that's in your own interests. You'll be more successful, more capable, happier if you adapt and learn at work, at home, in your relationships. And to do that, you have to be willing to listen to feedback that's intended to support you.

Part of being responsible is accepting that you're not perfect, that there's always more to learn, and that you can only improve if you listen to – encourage – feedback and constructive criticism.

I use the word constructive here because of course you'll encounter the odd person who gives you comments that are intended to put you down, or are trying to criticise your character. They'll make generalised remarks like 'You're so selfish', or 'You're rubbish with people'. You know when you hear these comments that they're not intended to help you learn, but to make you feel bad. Feel free to ignore these completely – that's the healthiest and most appropriate reaction. Criticism that isn't constructive isn't worth having.

> **THERE'S ALWAYS MORE TO LEARN, AND YOU CAN ONLY IMPROVE IF YOU LISTEN**

RULE 29

Be a good colleague

If you want to be successful and fulfilled in your work, you need to accept responsibility for your behaviour and for your actions. In terms of behaviour, you need to be honest and straightforward with your colleagues, turn up on time, meet deadlines, and not to try to blame anyone else on the rare occasions when that doesn't happen. When things go wrong, you'll accept your share of responsibility for it. When they go right, you'll give credit to everyone else who deserves a share of it, and not try to hog all the praise. In return, your colleagues will inevitably respect you far more for this approach.

In terms of your actions, you're responsible for your decisions, your strategies, the quality of your work. That means aiming high, and continuously looking for ways to improve. It's a big ask, but you're a responsible Rules Player who wants to succeed – for yourself, your employer and any team members – so you'll step up.

If you lead your own team or department, you're responsible for the work-related welfare of your team members – the buck stops with you. You have control over their job satisfaction, their personal development at work, their training, their opportunity to learn from mistakes, their welfare, their ability to ask for help, their working environment, how well they understand their goals, the atmosphere within the team. If those things aren't as they should be, don't blame anyone or anything else. You have to sort it out because it's your responsibility. And that's good because it means you have the power to make it right.

You have a responsibility to your bosses too. It's no good moaning and blaming everything you don't like on them. You're free to leave, remember? If you're staying, it's because you've chosen to. So commit. Do your best for the organisation, stand up for them – in front of colleagues and outsiders. No bitching sessions over the coffee machine.

Yes I know not every employer is perfect, but you're a grown-up, and you have to take the grown-up route. If you're not happy, don't whinge to your colleagues or team members. It's fine to discuss it, and agree the best recourse, but don't just bitch. Then try to instigate changes constructively. If that ultimately hits a brick wall, you have the choice to stay or to go.

Once you accept responsibility for your work performance, and that of your team, you know you're in charge, at least of your little corner of the company. That means you can feel confident to make decisions, to see what you need in order to improve, to recognise what training would help you, or what opportunities you could grasp. This will all go to make you more creative and more productive, so both you and your employer will benefit.

> **DO YOUR BEST FOR THE ORGANISATION, STAND UP FOR THEM**

RULE 30

Have a social conscience

No man – or woman – is an island. We're all part of a wider world, and being responsible means accepting our part in that, and the obligations we have to it. Everyone has a slightly different set of values and priorities, but all Rules Players understand the importance of treating other people well, and treading lightly on the ground.

I know you didn't ask to be born, never signed up to these obligations, but that's responsibility for you. It's not always what you'd choose, but it does make sense, and you'll be happier in the long run if you accept it. You may not appreciate every little detail, but you'll do far better in life if you go with the flow. Besides, as a Rules Player, you believe in the principle of doing your bit to make the world a better place. So your conscience will be clearer – and you'll be happier – for doing what you believe to be right.

Almost every interaction we have – with other people, with society at large, with the natural world – has either a positive or a negative effect. So our responsibility is to aim for a positive effect every time. From nodding to a passing acquaintance in the street rather than ignoring them, through to supporting local shops, or travelling by train instead of flying to help the environment.

Every scenario is different, and of course there are times we don't shop local, or we travel by air. We all have different causes we believe in, too. However the aim is the same – to do what we believe is the best thing each time. It's easy to kid yourself that the thing you'd like to do is the best option, when deep down you know it isn't. So this is about listening to that deep down voice of conscience, not the excuses in your head.

This isn't a book about how to be virtuous. It's about how to be happy. Not everyone is happy living like a monk or a nun, renouncing worldly goods, and devoting themselves entirely to good deeds. It's great that a few people do that, but you don't have to be one of them. You can carry on living a normal life, but make sure that where you have choices, you listen to your conscience – even when you don't particularly like what it's saying – and always consider the impact you have on other people and on the world.

It's about the tiny everyday choices as much as the big decisions – whether to call a friend who's going through a tough time, how you can make your new colleague feel a bit more included, finding time to sign a local petition. And it's about not leaving it in the hope someone else will do it. If you know it needs doing, why shouldn't it be you that makes the effort or finds the time?

> **ALMOST EVERY INTERACTION WE HAVE HAS EITHER A POSITIVE OR A NEGATIVE EFFECT**

GIVING

One of the great things about putting yourself out for other people is that it comes back to you. I don't just mean that people will return the favour, although most of them will want to if you need it. I mean that the act of giving makes you happy in itself. It makes you feel like a good, decent, moral, generous, right-thinking person – which indeed you are – and that's a great feeling. It's a feeling that boosts your self-esteem and bolsters your confidence.

And you can add to that the response you often get from the other person. Any unsolicited thanks, appreciation, gratitude adds positively to your sense of self-worth. There are of course ways to give anonymously, or without the recipient realising you did it for them, and in these cases simply seeing the advantage it brings them does the same job. You'll get satisfaction from seeing them benefit regardless of whether they're aware of your involvement.

The other person's response isn't your motivation of course. If you're deliberately trading your actions for a return of some kind – thanks, a return favour, a reward – that's not giving. That's a transaction. There's nothing wrong with transactions but they don't fall into the category of giving and, in the context of *The Rules of Happiness*, that's because in a fair trade your own happiness isn't noticeably affected. Of course it's different if the transaction is very unbalanced – the benefit to them is far greater than to you – these things aren't always black and white. However, you'll know by whether your actions bring you that warm feeling that comes from genuine giving.

RULE 31

Giving comes in many forms

There are plenty of ways you can give, and plenty of beneficiaries of your generosity. For our purposes here they all count, so long as they make you happier. Some will add a drop while others may bring a flood of happiness, and all are worthwhile. And you'll be adding to someone else's happiness at the same time, so it's a win/win.

You might think that you have little to give, or very little money. But material things are only one possibility when it comes to giving, and many of the other options will mean more to the recipient and, by extension, will make you feel happier for giving them. We gain more satisfaction when we've made a bigger effort, or a greater sacrifice, for someone else. Suppose you spend ages picking out exactly the right present for someone you love, or maybe making them something that money can't buy. The feeling you get when they unwrap it, and recognise what thought you've put into it, is so much more rewarding than when you give them yet another scented candle or bottle of wine.

So don't imagine that giving necessarily has to involve parting with money. And you're not restricted to giving physical things either. If you want to give more, and increase the sum of human happiness along with your own, you can give your time, your thanks, positive feedback or encouragement, constructive suggestions . . . all of these are forms of giving. If you can't afford to give money to charity, maybe you can volunteer instead (don't let me stop you doing both if you'd like to). Spending time with someone who is lonely, teaching your friend's kids the finer points of football or watercolour painting, random acts of kindness towards strangers – all of these are forms of giving something of yourself for someone else's benefit.

Not to mention the fact that you almost certainly have skills you can share. As a writer, I try to give the benefit of what skills I have to friends who want help writing a press release or putting together a business plan. A good friend of mine is a builder and often comes home from work only to go out again and mend a gate for someone, or fix their leaky tap. Another is an accountant and volunteers as treasurer for a local sports club. Look, you're a Rules Player, I'm sure you're doing a lot of this already. But you'll get even more out of it if you're conscious that it should be making you feel good about yourself, as well as making your neighbour feel good about their tap no longer leaking.

And don't forget all the time, love and effort you give to your own family. Calling your dad to check he's OK, reading to your kids, listening to your partner at the end of a stressful day . . . just think about how much you give every day, and enjoy the warmth that comes from realising how much you've added to other people's lives.

> **WE GAIN MORE SATISFACTION WHEN WE'VE MADE A BIGGER EFFORT, OR A GREATER SACRIFICE, FOR SOMEONE ELSE**

RULE 32

The more you give, the more you get

Such a lovely Rule. There are so many ways this is true. For one thing, it's human nature to reciprocate, so if you go through life being generous and kind, that's how the vast majority of people will respond to you. Of course there'll be a few grumps, or people you catch at the wrong moment, but in the grand scheme of things people will instinctively treat you in much the same way you treat them.

That means that on an individual level the people you encounter will be generous to you. And on a bigger scale you'll benefit too, from making yourself a path through life where your friends and family and colleagues are supportive and giving. On top of that, as we've seen, your happiness will increase because giving does that for you, over and above how others treat you.

So this Rule means that you benefit hugely by giving to other people. Whether it's your time, a listening ear, love, attention, walking their dog, helping with admin, making them a cuppa – you're doing it for them and your own happiness is a by-product.

These are all things you don't run out of too, apart from your time, which I grant is finite. But you have enough love, kindness and attention to go round everyone because it expands to fill the need. I remember after my first child was born wondering how I'd find enough love for the next when I was giving all I had to the family I already had. But of course, when my next child arrived, so did the love I needed – and that's been repeated many times since, as you probably know for yourself. As Juliet said to Romeo: 'My bounty is as boundless as the sea, my love as deep; the more I give to thee, the more I have, for both are infinite.'

You might think this Rule is so obvious it's hardly worth stating, and I might agree with you, except that I know far too many people who just don't seem to get it. I'm sure you know a few too. People who think only of themselves and rarely put themselves out for anyone, because they just haven't grasped that it's in their interests too.

I've also known people who will do anything for their family, for example, but are unwilling to help work colleagues. However this Rule works everywhere – at home, at work, with your friends, with strangers. When your bounty is as boundless as the sea, you don't have to pick and choose who to bestow it on. Everyone can have a piece.

> YOU HAVE ENOUGH LOVE, KINDNESS AND ATTENTION TO GO ROUND EVERYONE

RULE 33

Let it drip

It's quite true that when you give, it makes you feel good. Sometimes you make a huge sacrifice and sometimes it's a tiny contribution, and the effect on you is likely to be in proportion to what you've given. But it all adds up. Enough little moments of giving feel as good as one big one. And the little moments are much easier to turn into habit. All those random acts of kindness dotted throughout your day form a constant drip drip drip that helps to keep your self-esteem thriving, and which you barely need to think about.

Having said that, if you do think about them, the effect is more noticeable. You don't have to think about them every time – they'll still make you (and other people) feel better – but the benefit to you is intensified if you're aware that you're giving, that you're adding positively to other people's experience.

So smile at strangers on the bus, help parents up stairs with a pushchair, ask cashiers how their day is going, thank delivery drivers properly. And that's before you even start on the people you actually know.

Even when you don't have time today to call or see a friend who's going through a rough patch, you can still send them a brief message of support. You can offer to do your neighbour's shopping for them even if you think they have it covered – they'll appreciate the thought and they can always say no.

Look, you know this works. I don't need to teach my grandmother to suck eggs.* The point I'm making is that if you consciously build as many acts of giving into your day as you can, you'll be happier for it, and so will everyone around you. It quickly becomes a habit and, if you're doing it consciously, the benefits

---

* Although obviously if she'd like me to I'll be very happy to help

are intensified. You don't just feel good about each individual act of giving, you also feel good about the generous kind of person that you are.

> **ENOUGH LITTLE MOMENTS OF GIVING FEEL AS GOOD AS ONE BIG ONE**

RULE 34

Choose your charities

There may be countless ways in which you can give to others, but sometimes it's specifically your money which is wanted. Your limited funds. There's a lot of need in the world, sadly, and almost all charities are supporting genuine and worthwhile causes. However, that doesn't mean you can afford to give to them all.

Many charities find themselves in a position where they're effectively competing with others. The effect this has on you is that you can sometimes feel guilt-tripped into giving to a particular cause. That's because you care, and are moved by the suffering or damage that could be alleviated if only the charity had more money to spend. Sometimes you might watch television appeals where you're being asked to help exceed last year's total. Or someone stops you in the street, or rings your doorbell, asking you to sign up a small but regular amount for their good cause.

However, you still only have a finite amount you can spare, no matter how generous you're able or willing to be. So how can you navigate your way through all the requests and the emotional pressure, and give what you can without spreading your resources too thinly?

I've watched many friends and family grapple with this, and talked to people about how they give what they can without feeling bad about what they can't give. The broad principle that works is to think about it. Rather than reacting to requests ad hoc, the people who seem most comfortable with their charitable giving are the ones who have decided in advance what causes they want to support, and stick to that. They might put a few coins in a collecting tin, but anything they give above loose change has been thought through carefully.

I know people who focus their giving on wildlife, or on the homeless, or children, or refugees, or eco-charities, or veterans, or cancer research, or dogs. They pick a particular area and focus on that. Some have a couple of categories of charity, but they're chosen with care because of a particular interest or personal experience. We all choose differently, so there's plenty to go round all those worthwhile causes.

Beyond this, some people choose to support the big charities who have a lot of clout in their field, and others like to pick smaller charities where their own contribution will make more of a difference. Some prefer to give locally, others to charities with a broader remit. Again, the important thing is to think about it, and perhaps even research what opportunities are out there for giving in the field you care most about. Then make a donation, or set up a standing order, and find the best way to give what you want to a cause that really matters to you.

The result of this process is that next time you're asked for money for a cause that isn't your own, you can say with honesty, 'I've already committed my charitable giving for this year' or 'I've focused my giving on a different cause'. And because it's true, you can decline this request comfortably, knowing that your chosen charity is getting the benefit when you politely turn down others.

> **THE PEOPLE WHO SEEM MOST COMFORTABLE WITH THEIR CHARITABLE GIVING ARE THE ONES WHO HAVE DECIDED IN ADVANCE WHAT CAUSES THEY WANT TO SUPPORT**

RULE 35

Don't expect others to be indebted to you

I had a friend once whose family was pretty wealthy. Her parents gave money to her and her siblings from time to time. All very nice, you'd think. However, sometimes they would give to some siblings and not others, because they didn't like the way they'd spent the last lot of money. They disapproved of my friend selling her house to move abroad, so they cut her out of the next round of financial gifts.

Now I know that any kind of money sounds better than none, but my friend was really messed up by this. It felt as though her parents' love was conditional, given they treated her siblings differently. But these Rules aren't about the receiver, they're about the giver – that's you – and this is an example of when giving doesn't actually bring you the happiness it might.

Where gifts – financial or otherwise – have strings attached, they're not really gifts. That's a transaction in which the giver is trading money for power, and wants to exert control because the recipient is indebted to them. This is fine if it's all up front – there's nothing wrong with giving someone money for a specific stated purpose, such as a house deposit or uni expenses, and then feeling irked when they spend it all on sweets. However if you haven't agreed a particular use in advance, you're just taking advantage of their situation to control them.

I've seen this too often with grandparents, who give their children money, and then think it gives them the right to dictate how their grandchildren are raised. Again, I'm not talking about gifts given for a specific purpose, but emotional blackmail along the lines of 'When we gave you that money we didn't expect you to spend it all on holidays/we assumed you'd make sure the kids had piano lessons/we thought you'd spend more time with us'.

Once you have given someone a gift, it belongs to them. Unless it's been overtly agreed otherwise in advance, you have no further rights in the thing. Suppose you give your old car to your sister or your friend when you buy a new one. It's a generous thing to do, but you undermine all that if you complain when they trade it in three months down the line.

Whether you're giving time or money or anything else, if you want to come out of this happier – and you want to add to the recipient's happiness – make sure you're not building in unnecessary conditions in order to wield control, either through emotional blackmail or by withholding any future gifts. Otherwise you're not really giving, you're manipulating, and we Rules Players don't do that.

> **ONCE YOU HAVE GIVEN SOMEONE A GIFT, IT BELONGS TO THEM**

RULE 36

Let people be themselves

We're all different. I have friends who are really fit and healthy, and others who could really do with a much more health-conscious regime.* Some people always try to cram too much into their day, and others seem so laid back they hardly achieve anything. I know parents who spend way less time with their kids than they could, and grown-ups who rarely bother to visit their parents.

All these people have reasons for being the way they are, and I don't necessarily know what those reasons are. Sometimes they don't know themselves. I have friends and family who operate so differently from me in some regards that it seems to make no sense. But that's how they are, and it's far more productive and interesting to consider why, rather than try to change them.

This Rule follows on from the last one in some ways, but it goes well beyond that. One of the things that most people are very generous in giving is advice. Indeed it can be enormously helpful, and in my life many people have been hugely generous to me in passing on invaluable thoughts, ideas, information, guidance. But – and it's a big but – I've also felt quite pressured by people trying to make me do a certain thing their way when I know it just won't work for me.

Why won't it work? Perhaps it's a solution that works better for someone with other skills, a different personality, more time, different priorities, other enthusiasms. For example my friends who keep fit by running might advise me to do the same, but they love running and I hate it. I had two friends renovating houses and one kept telling the other they needed to be getting on with this or that before the bad weather set in. However the other friend wanted to take their renovation more slowly – they were a less driven personality and wanted to enjoy the process differently.

---

* Yes, alright, I mean me

Of course some people are happy to thank you politely for your advice and then ignore you. However it's easy to put someone under pressure without realising it, and that's when you're no longer giving – you're making things harder for them. Perhaps they feel rude disregarding you, or maybe it makes them feel they're doing things 'wrong' or 'badly'. Whatever the reason, all you're giving them is stress and pressure.

The safest policy to follow when it comes to advice is don't give it unsolicited. Wait to be asked. If the other person doesn't realise you have useful experience or knowledge you can always say, 'I know a bit about this' or 'I've been through something similar', and then let them ask you to elaborate if they want to. It's not a big deal if they're wondering what brand of cat litter to buy, but when it comes to anything important, people are constrained by who they are, and their constraints won't be the same as yours.

> **WAIT TO BE ASKED**

RULE 37

Don't overdo it

People who are willing to give their time, a listening ear, a shoulder to cry on, are a joy, and as Rules Players we should all want to fill that role when it's needed. When people are going through any kind of emotional turmoil, from break-ups to bereavement, nightmare bosses to serious illness, there's all sorts of help they might want.

Might want. Or might not. There are lots of reasons why someone might not want your help, and this Rule is about being open to that possibility. One of my family, who went through a particularly difficult period in her life, found that lots of friends offered support and help – for which she was very grateful. However she felt the need to prove to herself that she could cope, and didn't want to feel helpless, so she declined some of the offers because feeling capable was good for her confidence and self-esteem. Most of her friends were absolutely fine with this, whether they really understood it or not, and let her know they were there if she changed her mind.

However, there were occasions when friends wouldn't take no for an answer, or insisted on doing things for her even when she'd tried to tell them she could manage by herself. This made her feel she came across as less capable than she felt. It also meant having these friends around 'helping' on occasions when what she really needed was a bit of time to herself. You might question whether these friends really were giving, in the sense we've been talking about, if they left her feeling less happy. I'll let you ponder that one.

Another friend, who went through a particularly difficult divorce, told me he was hugely frustrated by people who followed what he called the false logic of 'You need to talk to someone . . . I'm someone . . . therefore you need to talk to me'. He recognised that talking things out might be helpful, but only with people that felt right, at a time that felt right. When you think about it, it's quite hard to find a polite way to tell someone in that situation that they're not the person you need.

So this Rule is about being sensitive to the fact that it's not helpful to give people things they don't actually want, and to be able to take no for an answer. Don't assume that someone necessarily needs to talk or that, if they do, you're the one they need to talk to. I appreciate that people sometimes decline an offer they'd really like to say yes to – for all sorts of reasons – and you may need to read between the lines.

However, in my experience the people who tend to foist unwanted help on their friends are oblivious to what they're doing. Their hearts are in the right place, but they're just not listening. If you're aware of the possibility, and looking out for the signs, you'll be able to read the situation sensitively. Having this level of empathy will make you an especially valued friend, which is a recipe for everyone's happiness.

> **BE ABLE TO TAKE NO FOR AN ANSWER**

RULE 38

Say thank you nicely

One of the most welcome ways you can give to people – at no financial cost – is with warm words. Thanks cost nothing, and nor do compliments, but they can have a significant impact if you deliver them in the right way. I know that all sounds a bit schmaltzy, but that's not how it will feel if you follow a few simple guidelines.

The first thing is that your thanks or praise must be genuine, or it will come across as disingenuous. I know someone who greets all women with, 'Gosh, have you lost weight?' which is intended as a compliment (I'm not sure it is) but is clearly not genuine because she always says it. So if you want to say something nice, make sure you mean it and it will come across as honest.

There's no point in a cursory thank you except for politeness. It's fine when someone hands you a drink, or offers you a chair, but if you want your words to mean anything, make them specific. That shows you've thought about them, so they must be true. I'll give you some examples:

- That was a delicious meal, thank you. I've never thought of putting thyme in it, and it goes perfectly with the lemon.

- I'm so grateful you looked after the kids for me. It must have been exhausting, but it meant I could catch up with all my admin, which is such a relief.

- I do like your outfit – you're so good at putting colours together.

- The reason this project was such a success was down to your exceptional eye for detail, coupled with the way you encourage people to co-operate with each other, so everything runs smoothly.

I hope you can see how anyone you say this kind of thing to will feel a real boost, because you've shown genuine appreciation. And that, in turn, should make you feel good about yourself.

All kind words are worth taking thought over, but if this is a big thanks, or significant praise, consider how the person on the receiving end is likely to feel best. For example, some people will really value being complimented in front of other people – maybe a specific other person (such as their boss, or their mother-in-law). Others hate being the focus of attention and much prefer a private thank you. The timing might make a difference to them, as will any kind of thank you gift. Forget the petrol station cellophane flowers – what would they really appreciate?

Next time someone makes you feel good with thanks or praise or compliments, take a moment to think about why it felt good, and what tips you can pick up from it. It's likely to have something to do with all the things we've just covered – it's personal, honest and specific – and you might also note a handy turn of phrase here, or a carefully chosen moment. You'll enjoy practising it yourself on someone else when the occasion arises, and it will give both of you a lift.

> **THANKS OR PRAISE MUST BE GENUINE, OR IT WILL COME ACROSS AS DISINGENUOUS**

RULE 39

Be accepting

We've just established that thanking and complimenting people adds to your own sum of happiness by making you feel good about yourself. So the logical progression from there is that others similarly feel better for giving you a thank you or a 'well done'. So why not give them the best possible response? You can feel better for making them feel good about making you feel good. It's a win/win/win.

The reasoning here may sound convoluted, but the reality makes complete sense. How you feel when you thank or praise someone is related to how they respond. It should always be a good feeling, but how good? Suppose you tell a friend that you like their new coat. Only a little thing, but here are two possible responses they might make:

- Thanks

- Oh good! I was worried it might look a bit outdated, so I'm glad you approve

Which of these will make *you* feel better for having commented?

When someone says something to make you feel good, they'll get more of a buzz from it if they can see it worked – that you do indeed feel better for their comment. So practise accepting thanks, praise, kind words, in a way that makes the giver pleased they bothered. That way everyone gets a positive emotional boost.

One good friend of mine doesn't seem to like being praised. They feel they should always be modest so if you thank them for the meal they just cooked you, they'll say 'Oh it's just an old recipe'. If you tell them their garden is looking lovely they'll say 'It isn't really, there are too many weeds and I haven't deadheaded lately'. I understand why they do it, but it kind of leaves me wondering why I bothered to comment. If they said 'Thank you – it's an old recipe but I'm pleased you like it', I'd feel better. Likewise if they replied, 'When I look at the garden I just see all the things I haven't done, so it's really good to get a glimpse of it through your eyes', it would give me the feeling they'd appreciated my comments.

It's an interesting exercise to make a point of giving thanks or praise (where it's genuine) in line with the last Rule, and then to notice what responses you get in reply. Think about how each reaction makes you feel, and see what you learn. It's much more fun living a life where you get a warm feeling every time you give positive feedback to someone else, *and* every time they speak positively to you.

> IT'S A WIN/WIN/WIN

RULE 40

Let others give too

We've spent the last few Rules establishing that when you give – compliments, money, support, thanks, time, praise – it adds to your happiness. There's a pleasure in giving that works on many levels and makes you feel worthwhile. The more opportunities you have to contribute to other people's lives, even in small ways, the better you feel.

So spare a thought for the people who have very few opportunities to be helpful or generous. Maybe they have very little money to give, or no time to spare, or few skills that anyone wants, or they simply don't get the opportunity to give much. They'd love that warm feeling that comes from giving, they'd love to feel useful or worthwhile, but they rarely get the chance.

Wouldn't it feel good to help them find that satisfaction? So why not make a point of asking them for something that is within their capabilities, so they can feel useful and derive the same pleasure from giving that you do?

One thing almost everyone is happy to give, and costs them nothing, is advice. As we've seen, it isn't always wanted, but if someone actually asks for your advice or opinion it always makes you feel good. It gives you a sense of value. So if you know someone who doesn't often get the chance to help people, why not ask them for advice?

I remember when one of my elderly relatives reached the point where they needed a lot of looking after and couldn't do much for themselves let alone anyone else. One day I wanted to speak to someone with knowledge about a particular field, and they fitted the bill perfectly. So I phoned them and said, 'I wanted to pick your brains…'. I could hear the delight in their voice that someone actually had a use for them.

So I now make a point of asking such people for advice or opinions or information – even if I could have gone elsewhere – because I can see how much it means to them. Oftentimes they're a really good source of feedback, and they generally have time to talk. So it's a genuinely productive interaction for everyone, and we both get to feel good about ourselves.

The real icing on the cake here of course is when you practise thanking them properly too. 'I knew you were the right person to ask – you always come up with angles I hadn't considered' or 'You've got such a good eye and you're right, it would look much better like that'.

> ONE THING ALMOST EVERYONE IS HAPPY TO GIVE, AND COSTS THEM NOTHING, IS ADVICE

MINDFULNESS

The technique we call mindfulness is a centuries-old tradition in Buddhism and Hinduism. However this particular use of the word in the West is fairly recent. It was coined in the last century as a translation of the Buddhist word *sati*. Of course, direct translations are often impossible because there isn't a word in your language that gives you all the necessary nuance, and that's certainly the case here. Other possible translations include 'awareness', 'attention', or 'remembering' (but not in the sense of remembering the past – you see, a good example of how tricky nuance can be).

Anyway, somehow the word 'mindfulness' became the go-to word, and it combines elements of all those other possible translations. The concept really started to gain traction in the West about 50 years ago and has become increasingly popular since then. That's because there's a growing body of scientific research to show that it can really help people with depression, stress, insomnia, chronic pain, and countless other conditions and difficulties. While it's fair to say that not everyone finds it helpful, it can be a welcome antithesis to the mad rush of modern life.

Essentially, mindfulness is about building the habit of living in the moment by regularly practising a 'mindful' way of thinking. So it's a form of meditation, but one where you don't have to light candles and sit cross-legged (unless you'd like to). It is often incorporated into yoga, but it doesn't have to be. You can do it while you're washing up, or walking in the park. For many people, it helps develop a state of mind that makes you more resilient and therefore increases your happiness levels. I can give you a sense of it, and some of the Rules to follow, in the next few pages. Then if you'd like to embed it fully into your life as a form of therapy, you might want to enrol on a course or read a dedicated book to expand your understanding even further.

RULE 41

Know your roots

Having said that mindfulness has its roots in Eastern religion and philosophy, it's helpful to understand that it has evolved into something slightly different in the West, something that fits more closely with our Western outlook. That's only natural – ideas evolve when they come into contact with other ideas and other cultures. However if you want to adopt mindfulness into your daily routines, it's helpful to understand the changes.

Buddhists see *sati* – which we term mindfulness – as an essential part of achieving enlightenment. As such, it's about rising above the slings and arrows of daily life, and achieving a state where the everyday, the mundane, the physical are no longer the focus.* In Eastern philosophy this makes a lot of sense; however here in the West it has often been adapted to help us cope with day-to-day problems, not to move beyond them. Some purists find this frustrating, and you can see why.

However, anything that helps us to feel happier is a good thing in my book, and the Western version of mindfulness earns its place on that basis. Most of us aren't trying to separate ourselves from the mundane in order to achieve nirvana, but simply to find a way to appreciate our ordinary lives fully. In the West, that doesn't have to be incompatible with a good and moral life, as we Rules Players know. We don't all want, or need, to become unworldly in order to achieve happiness on our terms.

The thing is, many traditional mindfulness practitioners would argue that this means Western mindfulness doesn't go far enough. It may teach us to be calm, to relax, to focus. However the Eastern approach goes beyond that, and uses mindfulness to gain real insight so you can understand yourself better. It encourages you not to relish earthly pleasures, but to transcend them. Western mindfulness might suggest you really focus on the experience

---

* Apologies to Buddhists for any over-simplification

of eating, for example, in order to get the most out of it, which would be in direct contrast to the Buddhist idea of separating yourself from the mundane.

Of course there are lots of branches of Eastern philosophy, each with their own take on mindfulness, and just as many Western proponents with their own styles. So once you decide to adopt the practice to help you manage any negative emotions, and bring you more calm and happiness, there is bound to be a mindfulness approach that suits you. Look around, and do a bit of research, and you have the best chance of learning to be mindful in the way that works best in your own world.

> **ANYTHING THAT HELPS US TO FEEL HAPPIER IS A GOOD THING IN MY BOOK**

RULE 42

Get the basics right

Before I go any further, I'd better explain what mindfulness actually is, in case you haven't had much to do with it before. As I've said, there are lots of variations on the theme, but they all share the same foundation.

The idea is to take a few minutes during which you focus only on the present. You're going to concentrate on your body, and on the physical and emotional feelings you're experiencing, to the exclusion of everything else. It's trickier than it might sound, but that's OK. We'll look at the specifics in the next few pages.

You can sit in a quiet space if you like, but you could also do it while you're walking or in the bath or doing something else that doesn't take up any of your attention, such as knitting.* The important thing is that there are no distractions, so you won't be able to do it while holding a conversation, or doing your accounts (however mindless that might seem).

Having found your undistracted moment, you're going to practise the principles we're going to look at in a moment. How much time you spend is really down to you. If you've chosen to follow a particular programme it will very possibly advise you on this, and that advice might be anything from 5 to 45 minutes. The fact is that there isn't one answer, which is good news because you can experiment with what works for you, or fits into your lifestyle.

When you first start doing this, even five minutes will seem like a long time. So one option is to start small and build up the time you take. However, you might find that five minutes is just fine and you don't want to take any longer. Frequency is more important than duration. There's some evidence to show that, say, four 5-minute bursts are as beneficial as one 20-minute session. Obviously not if you spread them over a month, of course – that's

---

* Assuming you're much better at knitting than I am

where the frequency comes in. Aim for some kind of mindfulness exercise every day, and if that's easier for you to achieve for only 5 minutes, it will benefit you more than finding time for one half-hour session a week.

I can't teach you everything there is to know about mindfulness in a few Rules. That's not how it works, and I'm not a mindfulness teacher. What I'm going to do is to set out the underlying rules, the elements that are common to all mindfulness programmes, so you have enough understanding to experiment for yourself, see if it helps you, and research further if you want to.

The reason so many people are using these techniques is because they really do have the potential to make you happier, by keeping on top of stress, depression, anxiety, insomnia and many other emotions or conditions that can otherwise bring you down. So it's well worth giving over a few minutes of your day to being mindful.

> IT'S TRICKIER THAN IT MIGHT SOUND, BUT THAT'S OK

RULE 43

Breathe

The most universal starting point for mindfulness exercises is breathing. There are other important elements we can look at later, but every time you start an exercise you need to breathe. No, not just in the most basic sense of not passing out – you need to concentrate on your breathing.

There are lots of breathing exercises you could do. The details don't matter, it's all about the fact that you're focusing on something very immediate and physical, which takes enough of your attention that it's hard for your worries to find a foothold at this stage. Generally speaking, there's no need for you to breathe deeply or differently as part of your mindfulness exercise. It's just about being aware of your breathing, and focusing on it in order to shut out any unwanted thoughts.

You know perfectly well that when you're agitated or angry or upset, your breathing can become fast or shallow. We sometimes instinctively release that in the form of a sigh, or a long exhale. To be mindful, you want your breath to be (or become) normal and steady, and the aim is simply to be aware of it, to 'watch' it, so to speak. That keeps your mind on the present.

So here are just a couple of examples of breathing exercises, and remember it's not the exact exercise that matters, but the effect it has on your mind.

- Simply count your breaths. Focus on your breathing, pay attention to it, and follow your breath in and out. Count each inhale–exhale cycle as one, and aim to get to 10 without your attention wandering. It's surprisingly hard to focus for that long until you get used to it, so just practise until you can. Then maybe add on counting back down to zero again.
- Breathe in and out through your nose, noticing how your lungs expand and contract, and the gentle sound of the air passing through your nose. Continue until you're aware that you feel calm and more relaxed.

While there's plenty more to mindfulness, as we're going to see, breathing exercises have their place even without all the rest of it, once you are able to do them easily. Any time you're feeling particularly anxious or emotional – the kind of scenario where people classically say to you 'Relax, just breathe . . .' – you can do a quick mindfulness breathing routine and it will help calm you. Before an important interview, or a big presentation, or getting on a plane, or launching into a difficult conversation.

> **THE AIM IS SIMPLY TO BE AWARE OF IT, TO 'WATCH' IT, SO TO SPEAK**

RULE 44

Observe

Once you've observed your breathing, and you're feeling a bit more relaxed, the idea is to take note of everything that is immediate and present. For example you might move your attention from your breathing to the rest of your body. You can do this with your eyes open – indeed that's not a bad idea if you're going for a walk – but if you're sitting or lying in a quiet space you might find it easier with your eyes closed.

Simply observe which parts of your body can feel contact with the chair, or notice whether you feel a bit hot or cold, and how you can tell. Feel the position of your limbs, or be aware of a strand of hair brushing your face, or a breeze passing over your skin.

Again, there are lots of different exercises you might do here, and the point of all of them is twofold. Firstly, the fact that you're focusing specifically on the here and now helps to push other preoccupations out of your mind for a few minutes. You can't worry about the past, or plan the future, if all your focus is on the present. Secondly, you're starting to develop a level of detachment, in which you are simply an observer noticing these things. You're not trying to change them or interfere with them in any way. You're simply accepting how they are and moving on to the next sensation. That's going to be critical in the next couple of Rules.

I'll give you a couple of example exercises for this too but, once again, the important thing is not the specific exercise. It's about focusing on the present, and being a detached observer.

- Focus on your senses. You're a detached observer, remember, so you're just noticing something you can see that you might not normally notice. A chink in the curtains, or the shape of a particular tree. Now become aware of what you can hear – again observe sounds you might normally not be aware of, such as traffic in the distance. Now what can you feel – the physical sensation of your clothes touching you, or the chair you're on. What can you smell? What can you taste? Obviously you can observe more than one thing for each sense if you want to keep the exercise going a bit longer.

- Find a flower, or a leaf, or pick up a book – the exact object doesn't matter, although something timeless and natural might feel calmer. Now just observe it for a few minutes, noticing things you normally wouldn't. Focus on the weight, the shape, the texture, the feel, the colours or patterns.
  Aim to make this object the only thing in your mind as you observe it.

These exercises are helpful in training yourself to be more mindful, and you can do them (or others like them) as part of your daily routine. And they can also be very helpful to bring a sense of calm if you start to feel emotional at almost any time during the day. Even if you have only a couple of minutes, they will help to bring you back to a more relaxed state.

> **YOU'RE STARTING TO DEVELOP A LEVEL OF DETACHMENT**

RULE 45

It won't always work

On one level, these exercises sound pretty straightforward. How hard can it be? The answer is that it's actually pretty hard. It's easier to focus without getting distracted when it's just a short time, as you'd expect, and the more you practise, the easier it becomes. Nevertheless, it's impossible to achieve total focus throughout, every time, unless you're already most of the way to enlightenment. It's especially tricky if part of your reason for practising mindfulness is that your mind is already overfull with thoughts that you find hard to stay on top of.

It's really important to understand this because it's inevitable your thoughts will intrude at times, and you need to recognise that it doesn't mean you're doing it 'wrong'. It just means that you're still learning. You expect to wobble about when you're learning to ride a bike, and sometimes even fall off. That's just a part of the learning process.

Similarly, your mind needs to be trained to focus on the present, and that takes time. So if you set out to be mindful and observe your breathing, and you suddenly notice that you're planning tomorrow's work schedule, just observe that you've shifted focus away from your breathing, and then go back to observing your breath flowing in and out.

Over time, you'll get better at distancing yourself from any thoughts that distract you, and just letting them go while you get back to focusing on the present. Don't be frustrated or annoyed with yourself for getting distracted because not only is it a natural part of the process, but also those responses will take you further away from your mindful state. Just acknowledge those thoughts, and slide off them and return to your present-moment ones.

If you think about it, although the thought might be about something in the future or the past, or elsewhere, the thought itself is happening here and now. And isn't that what you're supposed to be focused on? Aim not to be distracted by the content of the thought – yesterday's tricky conversation, or how you're going to navigate tomorrow's meeting – but the fact of the thought, that it's happening now, is a thing to observe. 'I can hear the fridge humming, I can smell coffee, I'm having a thought about tomorrow's meeting, I can feel my socks are slightly tight . . .'. There's nothing wrong with that. Indeed, as a detached observer, it puts the problems of tomorrow's meeting into an objective perspective that can be very helpful.

This is the detachment that you're ultimately aiming for. Yes, mindfulness exercises can be incredibly useful in themselves for grounding you when your more negative thoughts and feelings are starting to take hold. But on a wider level, you want to be able to bring the same detachment to your own emotions and moods as you do to the hum of the fridge or the smell of coffee.

> **THE THOUGHT ITSELF IS HAPPENING HERE AND NOW**

RULE 46

Don't stop thinking

It's true that mindfulness is a kind of meditation in a broad sense. However don't be misled into thinking that the aim is to empty your mind. In some forms of meditation you might be trying not to think about anything, but that's not what mindfulness is about.

The idea, as we've seen, is to cultivate a detachment – an objectivity – by taking a back seat and just observing what is going on in your mind. You might be noticing your breathing or the sensations around you, and equally you might be observing your own thoughts.

The mindfulness Rules we've looked at so far have been the basis of the thing. They will train you to focus in the right way on the present, and they can be a really effective quick fix when you need one, or a frequent go-to in order to stay on top of your day.

However, mindfulness can play a greater role in helping you to stay happy if you also use it to achieve the same distance and detachment from your own thoughts. As we saw at the end of the last Rule, thoughts can come to you unbidden when you're trying to do some other exercise. However once mindfulness becomes more of a habit, you can deliberately start to observe your own thoughts.

To begin with, it might be easier to do this when you're sitting or lying down and can dedicate a few minutes to it. Here's an example:

- Start by observing your breathing, and then extend out to observe the sensations around you.
- Once you have relaxed into your mindfulness headspace, start allowing your thoughts to wander. Just watch them, and allow them to drift, without joining in.
- If you realise that a thought has caught your attention and is taking you off somewhere, gently let go of its hand and go back to your observing role.

Over time, you'll be able to apply this strategy at random moments when you happen to experience a thought or a feeling that you don't want. When your brother makes a comment that leaves you feeling put down, or a work deadline is looming that you're not sure you can meet, or when the cat pees on the sofa. It will become much easier to stand back and observe your reaction, while keeping a part of your mind that acknowledges it without getting involved.

The idea is not to become numb to your emotions, or to become so detached that you are no longer a part of them. That might be closer to what some of the Eastern adherents are striving towards, but we're just looking for ways to be happier more of the time, and even one degree of separation from negative thoughts is a big step towards that.

> **WE'RE JUST LOOKING FOR WAYS TO BE HAPPIER MORE OF THE TIME**

RULE 47

Stay detached

Ready for the next Rule? Once you start to allow thoughts to drift past you in your mindful state, you need to stay detached from them. That means no passing judgement on what comes into your head.

It's easy to notice a thought and think 'I did that really badly' or 'It was her fault' or 'I need to take more exercise' or 'I hate that' or 'I love these'. However, if you do that, you're getting involved, and the aim is to remain detached. Try to observe those thoughts dispassionately, and notice that a particular thought is frustrating or guilty or blaming, or indeed happy. As you can imagine, this takes some getting the hang of, because in a sense you're in two minds at once – the one having the thoughts, and the one observing those thoughts (and of course those observations are in themselves thoughts).

So no, it's not always simple, and staying separated from some of your thoughts will be hard. However, if you understand what you're trying to achieve you should find with practice that it not only becomes easier but it also becomes really helpful.

The problem with judgements is that they limit you. Without realising it, we restrict ourselves by labelling ourselves, other people, activities, things, in ways we come to accept as facts. But they aren't facts. 'I have no self-discipline when it comes to exercise' or 'She's really tricky to work with' or 'I hate going to the movies alone' or 'You can't put peanut butter and jam in the same sandwich'. These are simply opinions – judgements – and they may not be right at all.*

Over time we become fixed in these views, and closed down in our thinking and our choices as a result. Being mindful is about

---

* Especially the peanut butter and jam. I resisted it for years, but turns out it's delicious – something to do with the salt and sweet combo

being in the present, without the baggage of the past – the place we formed these views. Watching your thoughts mindfully, without judgement, means you notice yourself thinking 'I haven't been for a walk in days' and you discard any of your usual thoughts about not having enough self-discipline. The only real fact is that you haven't been for a walk.

If you're prone to judge yourself harshly, you can learn over time to stop going instinctively from cancelling a social meet-up to 'I'm a rubbish friend' or from skipping a walk to 'I have no self-discipline'.

> **THE PROBLEM WITH JUDGEMENTS IS THAT THEY LIMIT YOU**

RULE 48

Open up

Of course it's human nature to judge. However when you learn to stop making judgements, you open yourself up to new possibilities. You could try peanut butter and jam if you have no judgement about it, and you might find you love it. Equally you might recognise your own preconceptions about working with that 'tricky' colleague, and get together on a project that could be really productive.

Learning to see judgements for what they are – just opinions that may not be factually correct – opens you up to all sorts of possibilities that can make your life less stressful and more enjoyable.

For one thing, once you recognise judgements for what they are, you can make better decisions. Rather than write a thing off, you consider whether your view of it is accurate. Even if it is, are you judging how much it matters accurately? A classic example of this is people who are looking to buy a house or rent a flat. You might insist that it has to face south and catch the sun. However, if you recognise that as simply a judgement about what makes for a good house, you'll be able to question whether it really is essential, or whether it's worth viewing other properties.

Even if, on analysis, you decide that south-facing is preferable, that doesn't mean it has to be essential. You might find a west-facing property with big windows and lots of light that is just perfect. And you'd never have viewed it without acknowledging that being south-facing was a preference, not an essential – the result of a judgement, not a fact.

Judgements can also have a big influence on your emotions. If it's grey and rainy and you think it will go on all week, you're likely to feel more negative than if you've seen a forecast that says the sun will come out in an hour or two and the week will be warm and dry. It's still grey and rainy now, in this moment, but you're allowing your mood to be influenced by what you believe will happen in future.

If you're running late, you can be stressed and late, or calm and late. You can't change what's going to happen, but if you focus on the present you can make now better. In the same way, if you assume that your upcoming meeting will be tricky, you'll be more anxious than if you believe it will be straightforward. The only difference is how you feel now – the meeting will be what it will be. Sure, prepare the meeting for all eventualities, but why ruin now?

Of course you can take some of these Rules on board without practising mindfulness, and that's fine. However mindfulness is a specific technique for incorporating this kind of thinking into your life, so if you can see the value of the Rules, you won't find an easier way to incorporate them into your life.

> **IF YOU FOCUS ON THE PRESENT YOU CAN MAKE NOW BETTER**

RULE 49

Retain your values

I hope you can see that once you learn to observe your own thoughts without judgement when you practise mindfulness, it's a fairly short step to withholding your judgement the rest of the time too. When something happens that makes you think, 'I don't fancy that' or 'I'm an idiot' you'll soon begin to recognise that you're having a thought that limits you in some way.

It's another good example of how, with practice, mindfulness can find its way into everyday life and help you find happier ways to deal with all sorts of situations. It doesn't mean you never form an opinion. It means that *when* you form an opinion, you acknowledge that's what you're doing, and only do it if it actually makes good sense.

In any case, a life entirely without judgement isn't necessarily a good thing. We don't want to dispense with judgements such as 'murder is wrong' or 'standing in front of a speeding train is dangerous'. These are judgements too, but most of us would be reluctant to live in a world where they're dismissed as merely opinions that limit us.

So you have to know which judgements you'll aim to overlook because they aren't helpful, and which you'll stick by because they're worth holding on to, even if they are just opinions. Remember those Buddhist practitioners of *sati*? They also follow the Buddha's teachings, such as being kind, generous, compassionate. However, those can be judgements too – 'That was a kind thing to do' or 'I could have been more compassionate'. So how come that's OK?

The clue is in the title of this Rule, as you'll have realised. It's helpful to let go of judgements that limit you or hold you back, but that doesn't mean you have to let go of your values. If you follow an organised religion such as Islam or Christianity or Judaism, those belief systems will bring their own moral principles to follow. If you're atheist or agnostic, you will likely hold similar values and follow your own moral compass. You're a Rules Player after all, and that comes with some pretty solid standards to aim for.

It's still helpful to acknowledge that these are judgements you're making – it's always helpful to identify your thoughts – and it's also fine to tell yourself 'This is a judgement that I'm happy to make because it's integral to my values and beliefs.'

> YOU'RE A RULES PLAYER AFTER ALL, AND THAT COMES WITH SOME SOLID STANDARDS TO AIM FOR

RULE 50

Feel your emotions

As we've seen, mindfulness can help you avoid self-criticism when you're going through difficult emotions. It can also help you take a step back from pain, or from anger, anxiety, depression or stress. These are not bad feelings in themselves – your anger may be justified, your anxiety may be justifiable. However, they're not pleasant feelings and you'd rather not have them.

It's easy to get caught up in these unpleasant emotions, and to get stuck in a pattern where they become compounded and lead on to other negative emotions – for example when you catastrophise and imagine all the bad things that might follow on (but also might not).

When you're going through this kind of negative experience, try to take a few minutes to practise mindfulness. Obviously you may not be able to do this immediately, depending on the circumstances, but get a few minutes to yourself as soon as you reasonably can. Always start by getting comfortable, and finding the right headspace by focusing on your breathing and the sensations around you.

Next, allow yourself to feel the emotion in question, but take no notice of any other feelings around it. So if you're focusing on your anger, for example, ignore any related feelings such as blame or guilt. Simply feel the anger, and observe yourself feeling it without any judgement.

Shift your focus to your body, and make yourself aware of the physical changes that this emotion is bringing. Are there areas of tension? Of heat or cold? Are your shoulders slumping? Is your heart rate faster or slower than usual? Are you sweating? Or feeling a knot in your stomach? Just observe these things, and notice whether they change while you're watching them.

Generally we try to stop ourselves experiencing negative emotions, although we all know that doesn't necessarily work. In fact that kind of focus can make them worse. Using mindfulness, you're not trying to stop the emotion, you're allowing it to happen while you observe it. You're giving it permission to exist, without judgement of course, and without trying to change or manage or analyse it. Sometimes that is enough in itself to allow it to dissipate.

Once you have explored this emotion, you can start to observe any other emotions that are running alongside it. Guilt, hurt, sadness, frustration. Go on, take a look at them without getting involved. Separate them from the core emotion you're dealing with so they don't get compounded and over-complicated.

Obviously this isn't a magic bullet – there's no such thing – and you can't magic away all your unwanted emotions in ten minutes. However it can make really useful inroads into strong feelings, and the more you practise it, the more helpful it becomes.

> **YOU'RE NOT TRYING TO STOP THE EMOTION**

TIME

Much of our happiness is determined by what we do with our time, and whether those things are enjoyable. It's hard to be happy when you feel most of your waking life is spent in activities you don't enjoy, or can't enjoy because there's too much to cram in to be able to savour the good bits.

On the other hand, there's a huge satisfaction to be had from feeling you're in control of how you spend your day, and can give the time you want to the things you care about. Of course there will always be chores and essentials that you'd rather not be doing right now, and it's unrealistic to aim for a life with 24 hours in every day to do with as you will. However, you can create a balance where there is enough time for the things that matter, and you can relax about getting everything else done.

Even when you have to find room for work, kids, shopping, laundry, cleaning and all the rest of it, it should still be perfectly possible to use your time in ways that increase your happiness, rather than impinge on it. It's about understanding the role of the things that occupy your time, and using that understanding to maximise the positive and make your time work for you.

RULE 51

Chores are necessary

Most of us are inclined to think that we'd be much happier – and have far more free time – if we didn't have so many chores to deal with. From work emails to doing the laundry, a lot of our day involves tasks we don't particularly enjoy and which take up time we'd rather spend some other way.

It's true that doing the weekly shopping will never have the same appeal as the activities you do from choice. Few people would willingly prioritise changing the bed sheets over spending time with their friends, or at their favourite hobby. Surprisingly, though, if you removed all these little chores and routines from your life, it would be unlikely to make you any happier. In fact, you'd probably just replace them with others.

Experiments have shown that if you put people in an environment where there are no routines of any kind, they create them. We need these punctuation points throughout our day and our week to create an anchor, and give us a sense of control in our lives. Even a sense of purpose. When this structure is taken away, we feel adrift and unsure of ourselves, and uncertain about how we can manage. It's not that we enjoy the washing up, but it's not difficult. It's a few minutes that don't tax our brain, and it is at least familiar – we're on safe, if unexciting, ground.

When you think about it, this is part of the reason we adopt the habits we feel we've chosen, the ones that make us happier in at least some small way. Maybe you always sit down with a cup of coffee and a newspaper before you start your day, or go to the gym every morning, or eat lunch in the park, or read to the kids every night before bed. Or perhaps you carefully cut a sliver of cheese and place it next to your cored and quartered apple on the plate just so . . . You enjoy these activities in themselves, but you also enjoy the habit, the routine, the familiarity, the punctuation mark in your day. Well you're deriving all those benefits from the chores you didn't choose willingly as well. The only difference comes in the precise nature of the activity.

So we might as well accept the chores. Of course there are times in our lives when there are genuinely far too many of them, or specific chores that we absolutely hate. I'm not suggesting that all chores are inherently a good thing in all circumstances. The principle stands, though, that we need routine and, while chores are not the only kind of routine, they're a very effective one for giving you a sense of purpose, and structure, and for notching your brain down a gear or two for a while. In other words, they actually contribute to our overall happiness in a roundabout way.

> WE NEED THESE PUNCTUATION POINTS THROUGHOUT OUR DAY AND OUR WEEK TO CREATE AN ANCHOR

RULE 52

Lean in

If we're not going to try to get rid of these fairly boring activities, then, we need to find ways to make them less frustrating so they don't interfere with our perceived happiness. For most of us, some tasks are dull but fine, while one or two really get to us. So consciously seek out strategies for improving those odd chores that really bug you. In fact, actively try to find joy in them.

For a start, you can be conscious of the fact that chores are not a bad thing in themselves. You can acknowledge the sense of the familiar, the reassuring routine, even when the activity itself isn't what you'd choose. You could even add to that by making the chore into *more* of a routine by standardising the time you do it every day or week. That way, you can follow it with something enjoyable, and the chore becomes the precursor to something positive. I have a relative with austism who works in a market garden. He often says to himself, 'First you must push the wheelbarrow, and then you can sit down'. In other words, pushing the wheelbarrow takes on a positive sheen because it means you get to sit down soon.

Once you resolve to be creative about leaning in to the chores, there are lots of ways you might make them tolerable, or even fun. You might even get out of them altogether . . . for example, I dislike shopping and my wife hates doing laundry, so when the kids were young we traded – she did all the shopping and I did all the laundry.

More often the solution lies in how I approach the task, when I can't avoid it altogether. I have chores that I don't mind if I can listen to music while I do them, or I amuse myself by timing them to see if I can break my record, or I do them with someone else so we can natter. Some people enjoy actually taking longer over a chore if that means they can make it look really neat, or in some other way derive satisfaction from having done it. Even putting out the bins is more fun if instead of thinking about dealing with yuk, you focus on creating a clean, unsullied kitchen.

When I have to shop, I buy myself some kind of little treat* – maybe conditional on keeping within budget. Then I pack it at the bottom of the bag so when I get home, it's my reward for unloading and putting away everything I've packed on top of it.

Don't resign yourself to being miserable for five minutes, or an hour. Remember that we all need chores, so look for ways to make this one at least bearable, or perhaps mildly diverting, and maybe even actively enjoyable.

> **ACTIVELY TRY TO FIND JOY IN THEM**

---

* I don't know why you're assuming it's chocolate

RULE 53

How you spend your day is how you spend your life

OK, so we can't get out of doing the chores, and we shouldn't try. However, the rest of the day is your own to do as you choose. Much of that time will be determined by choices you've already made such as to study, or have a job, or have children, or more than one of the above. These are ultimately all choices, some of which we have to live with, and others which we could change if we wanted to. Of course some of them are constrained by our abilities or experience or age, but there are always options involved.

The thing is, it all adds up faster than you think. It's easy to take a short-term job you don't particularly enjoy when you're 25, and still be doing it ten years later. It's no longer a stopgap, it's your life. If it makes you happy, that's fine. But don't drift along with the flow if you don't like it. Get out of the river. It's sad how many people keep telling themselves this is only temporary, or they're going to do that soon, and they never do.

The things that fill your regular days *are* your life, and if you don't like it, you need to do something about it right now. Whether that's your job, or where you live, or how you spend your free time. Don't keep telling yourself you're going to retrain, or start studying, or take up painting, or join the tennis club. If you're not actually doing it now, it simply doesn't count for anything. Of course you might have to wait until you start your new job before you can do this, or hang on until the kids are all at school before you do that. However, once that necessary milepost has passed, just get on with it.

This section is all about how the way you spend your time can add to your happiness. So recognise that time is finite. If you're 80 you won't need me to tell you that, but if you're still young, it's not always easy to see how the days and weeks turn into months and years, without you doing the things that will make you happy. What's the problem, anyway? Why aren't you living your dreams? Inertia? Can't stay off your phone long enough to do anything about it? Scared it won't work out? Haven't done the maths? So identify the barrier, and work out how to overcome it, or you'll still be here this time next year.

It's fine with me if you put this book down right now while you go and research courses, or look for a better job, or sign up to that activity. Literally. Because if you don't do it now, when will you do it? Tomorrow? The day after tomorrow? Next month? Next year?

You need to know what kind of life you want, what people and activities and achievements you want in it, and you have to start now. Right now. Otherwise you'll look back later and it won't be the life you wanted. And that realisation is not going to make you happy. Whether you've drifted for six months or for decades, you won't get that time back. Whereas if you do the things you really want to, and can look back on time well spent and forward to fun or exciting times ahead, that will be fulfilling and satisfying and will feel like a happy life.

> **DON'T DRIFT ALONG WITH THE FLOW IF YOU DON'T LIKE IT. GET OUT OF THE RIVER**

RULE 54

Strike the balance

We often talk about work/life balance as if we all need to finish work at a fixed time and then switch off and go home. And indeed that is the best approach for some of us in some jobs. Mind you, it's not how the world has worked until very recently, and there are still many places and people for whom it's a fairly alien concept.

You'll be hard pressed to find a farmer who knocks off at 6 pm sharp no matter what. Or a small business owner. Lots of people run independent shops, or market stalls, and don't buy into the whole concept of 'going' to work. Work and home become intertwined, deliveries turn up in the evening, customers come to the door, accounts get done after the kids are in bed, sheep need help lambing at 3 am, tomorrow's food offering has to be cooked this evening.

Fewer and fewer people in the West live this way. We work someplace away from home, and so our 'work' and 'home' lives become separated. For lots of people this all changed during Covid, when suddenly they had to work from home, perhaps fitting it around schooling their kids, and most of us got a taste of this kind of blended home/work existence. Some people hated it, and some took to it like a duck to water.

We're all different, and what suits one person doesn't have to suit the next. There's no fixed right way to do this, other than finding a balance that works for you, now. That might change in the future – if you get promoted, or have kids, or start your own business, or semi-retire – but you need to identify what you need right now, and then find a way to achieve it. It'll never be exactly perfect every single day, but it doesn't need to be. However if you're too far off balance, your life won't be as enjoyable as it could be.

If your balance isn't working, remember the last Rule and do something about it. Talk to your boss, change your job, adapt your business, find a workspace outside your own house, reduce your hours, negotiate to work from home more – or less. If you want to be responsible for your own happiness, and quite right too, this could be a big part of that. We all go through periods when the balance isn't quite right, and the people who are most determined to be happy do something about it.

Of course it's not always easy. There may be tough choices. If your boss won't budge, you'll have to choose whether to stay or go, and that can be hard. Or maybe you can find a way to adapt your home life to bring things into balance better – move house to shorten the commute, pay for help at home so at least you can relax when you're there – in the way you'd adapt your work life if you work for yourself. The key thing is to understand that you're the only one who can sort this out, so if it matters to you, you need to do something about it.

> IF YOU'RE TOO FAR OFF BALANCE, YOUR LIFE WON'T BE AS ENJOYABLE AS IT COULD BE

RULE 55

Find your happy place

We probably all do this on an unconscious level, but this Rule is about being aware of the little things that bring you peace. It might be a place or an activity or other people. Something that brings you back to earth – grounds you – and brings you joy even when your day, your week, your life are going awry.

You need to know what works for you, and find time to do it regularly. That will train your brain to drop into its happy state readily when you need it to, and the more time you can find to do the things that make you happy, the better.

For example, some people find sitting listening to the right music hits the spot. For others it's playing with the dog, going for a run, meditating, sitting in the garden, taking a long bath, reading a good book, watching comedy videos, dancing to music. Much of the value of these activities is that they keep you in the present. You don't have the brain space to worry about anything else while you're doing them. That's probably also true of, say, complicated algebra. However these activities are easy, relaxing and fun.*

You need a happy place that you can actively engage in, not just one that numbs you. That may mean avoiding phones and video games and the like for this purpose. I'm not saying you can't use them – just that they don't always tick this particular box. It depends how you use them and what you're doing. Ditto alcohol. So you may need something else to fit this Rule, something that actively makes you feel good, even when things are going badly. You're looking for a reliable happy place, not one that you need to be in a positive frame of mind to enjoy, because you want to be able to use it when you need it most.

---

* With apologies to any mathematicians for whom complicated algebra is their happy place

You also want something you can access easily. It's no good if the only place you can calm yourself is your favourite beach 250 miles away. That's not going to work on your lunch break, or between now and when the kids need picking up from school. So find something that is available any time, works in all weathers, and can be fitted into a 15-minute break if necessary. Obviously you can have more than one happy place, and they don't all need to be at your fingertips constantly, so long as at least one of them is there when you need it.

And here's the important bit . . . use it. When you're having a bad morning, or a rough week, remember that you have a happy place that will help to restore your spirits, and use it. If you only have five minutes it's not going to fix a nightmare day, but it will bring you back to a place of calm and put things in perspective. For example, I have a friend who copes with really bad work days by hiding for five minutes, in the office restroom if necessary, and listening to a favourite music track that either energises her, or calms her down, according to need.

> **MUCH OF THE VALUE OF THESE ACTIVITIES IS THAT THEY KEEP YOU IN THE PRESENT**

RULE 56

Don't get overstuffed

Some of us like to keep pretty busy, and some of us like to build some time into our diaries to fill – or not – when we get to it. That's fine, and you should do whichever works for you. However many of us go for a third option – pack your diary really full and then get stressed when you can't fit everything in, or keep cancelling things because you're exhausted.

This doesn't make sense when you think about it, but to judge by how many people do it, we don't always think about it. So if this is you, think about it now. An overfull diary doesn't make you happy, it makes you stressed. Just because there's a little blank space left on the page that looks free, it doesn't mean you'll have the time or energy when you arrive there in real life.

And actually, that's pretty stressful. Once you've committed to something, it's not a good feeling having to do it when you're not in the right headspace. Nor does it feel good letting people down, or missing out on a thing you hoped you enjoy. On the other hand, think how relaxing it is at the end of a long day having a clear evening to just chill, or how much better you cope with a busy week when you know your weekend will be restful.

So it's important not to fill your diary to bursting point, for lots of reasons. For one, you can't assume you'll have the energy just because it looks like you have a gap. For another, things come along that you didn't expect – you come down with a bug, the car breaks down, your child needs picking up from school because they're sick, water has started coming through the ceiling, the dog has to go to the vet urgently, the boss drops an unexpected load of work on your desk, your brother asks you to house sit while he's away. . . . It's no good complaining when this happens. You should have known it would – not this specific thing, but something unscheduled – because that's normal life. If you haven't allowed for it, that's your own fault.

But it's not about whose fault it is. It's about keeping you relaxed and enjoying life, rather than anxious and in a mild state of panic about how you'll get everything done. So take a long look at your diary and think about all the things in it that you are doing by choice – going for a run, socialising, walking your neighbour's dog, tap dancing lessons, being part of a local group or club, going to the movies, anything that takes up diary space. Those things are pushing out all the stuff you don't put in your diary – reading, tinkering with the car, gardening, watching TV, hanging out with the family – the stuff you were thinking about in the last Rule. If you're happier when you have time for the things in that second category, you need to remove some of the activities in the first group.

It's not enough to assume that everything will run smoothly and there'll be time for everything. There won't be. If you don't build in time to relax and chill, you're not going to get much opportunity to relax and chill. So don't bury your head in the sand and keep believing nothing will ever interrupt your smoothly planned day. You'll just be one of those manic people who overcommits and then lets everyone down at the last minute because 'something unexpected has come up'. It's not unexpected at all.

> **IF YOU DON'T BUILD IN TIME TO RELAX AND CHILL, YOU'RE NOT GOING TO GET MUCH OPPORTUNITY TO RELAX AND CHILL**

RULE 57

Prioritise regularly

I hope you're fairly much able to prioritise individual tasks when you have a full to-do list.* It's not always easy, and it's well worth honing the skills you need to stay in control of your time. However, that's only half the story. It's relatively straightforward to perfect the strategies to keep on top of your diary – including the last Rule among others. What takes more of a conscious effort is to step right back and look at how you spend your time in a broader sense.

We rarely do this, except at times of change. Maybe you start a new job with very different demands on your time, or your elderly parent moves in with you so you can help care for them, or you start a family, or the kids leave home. Those are the moments we tend to realise that something has to give, or indeed that permanent space has opened up in our week.

But why wait for these big life events or major incidents to run a mental audit on your activities? This is something you should be doing regularly – it should be in the back of your mind, ready to focus on every few months or every year or two. The fact is, it's easier to add things to your diary than to remove them, so that over time your commitments build up. When that becomes too much to cope with, the last Rule about not getting overstuffed should kick in. However, even when you're not at that stage of having a stressfully busy diary, you should still think about its overall balance.

This is about big life stuff. Not just finding time for your day-to-day happy places, but where are you, where would you like to be, how are you getting there? Are you spending enough time with your partner, your kids, your friends? Are there people in your life you'd like to draw back from? If you want to set up your own

---

* Incidentally, *The Rules of Success* has a whole section on how to manage your time effectively, focused in more detail on strategies for managing your diary

business, should you be making time to study or train? If you want to cut down on work, do you need to invest time in finding other ways to make ends meet? If you're ambitious for your career, should more time go into that? If you've always wanted to paint, is now the time to create the space, or the time, or enrol in classes?

Remember, this is all about what makes you happy. Are you putting your time into the things that make you happy now, or will make you happier in the future? And if not, what are you going to do about it? That has to be worth taking a good look at every so often to make sure you're still on track, and using your time in the best way for the long term. Get those key priorities right, and you're a long way towards living the life you want.

> **WHERE ARE YOU, WHERE WOULD YOU LIKE TO BE, HOW ARE YOU GETTING THERE?**

RULE 58

Drop your standards

One friend of mine spends hours every week keeping her house looking spick and span. That would be fine, except that she doesn't have hours every week to spare, so she stays up late cleaning the kitchen, or gets up early to vacuum. Why does she do this? It's because – she tells me – she can hear her mother's voice inside her head telling her it all has to be perfect.

I know it doesn't have to be perfect. You probably know it doesn't have to be perfect. In fact, she knows it doesn't really have to be perfect. But her mother's voice apparently feels otherwise. So my friend continues to run herself ragged sprucing up her house for an imaginary voice. And I can understand that, because the voices in our heads can be very powerful, and hard to argue with.

Rationally, however, it just doesn't make sense. My friend's mother will have grown up in a different era, with different standards, and perhaps without the demanding job my friend has. Even if that weren't the case, she's not the boss now my friend is a grown-up. In a good week, she'll be tired but she'll cope. In those weeks where things don't run smoothly, she'll either be exhausted, or she'll feel hugely stressed by any housework she hasn't managed to do.

In your case, it might not be housework,* but most of us have certain areas where we set our standards higher than they need to be – or at least higher than they need to be every single time, no matter what else is going on. Sometimes this doesn't matter, if it rarely arises or takes only a moment longer, but as you can see from my friend's example, it can significantly add to your stress levels. And it will do that specifically on those occasions when you're already stressed.

---

* It certainly isn't in my case

Some people like to clear their inbox every day, which is an admirable aim but there will be days when it puts you under unnecessary pressure. Or maybe you disapprove of any kind of fast or processed foods, so even after an exhausting day you won't countenance opening a tin but insist on cooking properly. Whether it's at home or at work, if these things add to your stress with any frequency, you need to face up to them if you want a more relaxing life. You might need therapy, you might need to give yourself a good talking to, you might even find that identifying the tendency is enough to stop yourself doing it. But once it starts to intrude on your life regularly, you need to address it in order to reduce the pressure on your time.

By the way, going back to my friend's example, while many of these overly high standards are self-imposed, some of them come from our parents. So if you have kids, try not to saddle them with your imaginary voice inside their heads for the rest of their lives, when they're overworked or exhausted and just want to leave the washing-up until morning.

> **THE VOICES IN OUR HEADS CAN BE VERY POWERFUL, AND HARD TO ARGUE WITH**

RULE 59

You control your phone

Well, the Rule is 'You control your phone' but does it feel that way? It's not just about the amount of time your phone – or other devices – occupy, it's about that feeling of being at its beck and call. Never quite being able to relax in case the boss messages, or an alert goes off, or someone calls. Once upon a time – after there were phones but before they were mobile – you could only be reached if you were in your house or at your desk. Anywhere else and you were free, able to relax knowing you were uncontactable. That's a feeling anyone under the age of about 30 or so has simply never experienced.

I may be an old fogey, but I absolutely get the benefit of mobile phones. There's a reason everyone wanted a phone about their person 24/7 once they'd been invented. Of course there are loads of upsides, but that doesn't take away from the downside of never quite feeling that you won't be summoned across the ether by someone or something that wants your attention. That makes complete relaxation really hard, and makes it hard to fully focus on anything else.

Some of us like it that way – or we think we do. Nevertheless it does something to your psyche because you're always in standby mode and can never fully switch off. That's not healthy. And obviously, when your phone is switched on, it can also be occupying your time. Time you could have spent in other ways. Without a phone to scroll through on your morning commute, you could have used the time to read a book or prepare for a meeting. If you weren't checking the phone in the evening, you might actually have heard what your partner was saying to you. Without that last check before bed – which is clearly going to take time if you find anything you want to respond to – you might have got a better night's sleep. So even if the time you spend on your phone isn't overloading your time, it still isn't the best use of it – which is to say, the use that brings you the most happiness.

What's the answer? It's not practical to throw away your phone, and anyway you'd lose the countless advantages it brings. However, it can make a big difference to switch it off a bit more often so it can't ping and buzz and ring. You can set it up to let through emergency callers – partner, parents, kids – but otherwise put it in sleep mode. Like you would in an important meeting, or at the cinema.

Pick the time of day you think it would benefit you most. For example, set it to wake up an hour after you do, and don't look at it during that time, so you have a relaxed hour to get up every morning. Or have a family rule you turn off your phones during mealtimes. Or switch off an hour before bedtime, or when you're together as a family.

Just because your phone isn't bleeping for your attention, it's not going to help if you look at it anyway. This is time when you can properly switch off, and it might take a bit of practice to stick to it. But once you do, the sense of relief should be palpable. You might find an hour a day does it for you, or you might want to add other quiet times to your day.

> **IF YOU WEREN'T CHECKING THE PHONE IN THE EVENING, YOU MIGHT ACTUALLY HAVE HEARD WHAT YOUR PARTNER WAS SAYING TO YOU**

RULE 60

Be ready to jettison

It's hard to be chilled and relaxed, to enjoy life, when you're starting to be overwhelmed by having too much to do. That might be true either at home or at work, or maybe even both. You end up with a constant background anxiety about your workload, waking in the early hours, scrawling yourself notes and reminders. The longer it goes on, the more it gnaws at you, and gets in the way of your happiness.

There are lots of specific things you can do to get on top of this kind of backlog.* If this is a scenario you find yourself in frequently you'll need to learn some strategies both for coping, and to prevent it recurring time and again. But sometimes it's not your usual modus operandi, and you're confident that if you can just get back on top of things somehow all will be well again. Either way, this Rule can be really useful.

As so often, part of this Rule is about remembering to use it. It seems obvious but you may need to think out of the box in order to make the most of it. The idea is simple – if you can clear just one really sizeable thing off your to-do list, everything else will fit comfortably. The trick is to realise you've reached this point, and then to be able to find the one thing you can remove.

I know someone who ran a business from home, and was becoming increasingly stressed and overloaded. Her problem was that she had too much on her plate. She was starting to get behind with her accounts, she was temporarily covering for a member of staff on top of her own work, and she couldn't get back on top of it all in the evenings as she usually would, because she had decorators in. The decorators were a problem because they couldn't paint any room until she'd cleared it for them, and the clear-out was long overdue and hugely time consuming. She'd worn herself out clearing the upstairs for them, but they were

---

*As I mentioned before, *The Rules of Success* looks at this in detail

going to move downstairs in about three weeks and she hadn't even started on that.

She talked to me about it, and couldn't see a way to get back on top of things without her accounts slipping too far behind along with the rest of her work. As we talked, I asked her what would happen if the decorators left the downstairs for a few months and came back when she was back in control at work, and able to continue the clear-out. I saw the light bulb go on behind her eyes as she realised that this would solve everything. I took the credit – of course – but in fact it's often far easier to see this kind of solution for someone else. The trick is to learn to do it for yourself, or of course to ask other people for ideas if that helps.

It can be a wrench when you were looking forward to a freshly painted kitchen, but it gives you a choice, and throwing out – or postponing – one big task can be the thing that makes everything else workable. It might be a home project like an extension or a garden renovation, or at work it might mean holding off on a project or delaying a round of interviews.

> **IT CAN BE A WRENCH BUT IT GIVES YOU A CHOICE**

CONNECTION

The biggest ever piece of research into happiness has been running since the 1930s, following people born into different levels of wealth or poverty in Boston (the study is run by Harvard University). Of course many of those people moved away from Boston, but the study has continued to follow them and their families and children, regularly interviewing them about their life and health.

The results have been fascinating over the years, and the standout discovery has been that good social relationships are by far the biggest factor in happiness, a finding that has been backed up by plenty of other research since. In other words, people who report that they have good relationships are happiest. They're also healthier and live longer. You might think that social background, or genes, or even IQ would be more important, but in fact those things are less reliable predictors of happiness than social connections.

Now contrast this. Other studies have shown that one in three people often feel lonely. What that looks like on paper is different for everyone, of course – some of those people may be living with a partner and live busy lives, while plenty of people who live on their own nevertheless have strong relationships and don't feel lonely at all. What it tells us, however, is that if you're serious about wanting to be happy – and who isn't? – taking stock of your relationships, and thinking about how and who you connect with, is central.

This next set of Rules should help you to do just that, putting your relationships at the centre of your life so you can be happier, healthier, and live longer to enjoy it.

RULE 61

Quality not quantity

It's very clear from many studies into happiness that social connection is the single biggest factor. Humans are a social species so that's not so surprising when you think about it. It also helps to explain why some people manage to be happy despite apparently having nothing, while others can be wealthy and successful and yet seem not to be happy at all. Of course your basic nature will be a factor,* but the real point is that happiness isn't about stuff, it's about people.

These days you can have countless 'friends' on social media, and you can encounter dozens of people a day in your job, or if you go to lots of parties or events. And certainly all those little connections add up and help you to feel connected in a broader sense.

However the connections that have the biggest impact on your happiness are the close ones – family and good friends, the relationships where you feel a sense of closeness. Even just one or two really strong, close relationships can make all the difference.

Interestingly, one study looked at married couples in their 80s, an age at which very few people escape general aches and pains, and many have significant health issues. The researchers found that when one of these people was in physical pain, their mood was correspondingly low if they were unhappily married. However those people who reported being in a happy marriage found their mood wasn't adversely affected by their pain level.

I find that particular finding really interesting, because it gives such a clear sense of precisely why these close relationships are so important. They really do affect your mood, and enable you to cope with life's ups and downs – they help you to be much more resilient.

---

* Along with how many of these Rules you're following

Look, it's great knowing dozens of people who you only interact with online, or who you pass in a corridor at work, or encounter in the street. But when it comes to your happiness, you also need really close relationships. You don't need many of them, but you want to spend time with people who you feel really understand you, and who you know have your back no matter what. People who would drop everything for you in a crisis, and for whom you'd do the same. That closeness is the thing that matters most, even if it's only there in a handful of your relationships.

> **HAPPINESS ISN'T ABOUT STUFF, IT'S ABOUT PEOPLE**

RULE 62

Make the time count

I have several friends who I meet up with occasionally one-to-one for a drink or a coffee. The conversation always goes the same way. I ask them what they've been up to, and then they ask what I've been doing since we last met. Next, I ask after their family and they give me a run down of their kids, their partner, siblings and so on – this one has moved house, or that one has changed jobs, or another one had a cold but they're better now. Then we go through my family (that can take a while). By then, a couple of hours have passed and we say how lovely it was to see each other and we must do it again soon.

On a surface level, of course there's some sort of connection going on here. The fact we bother to meet shows that we care about each other, and we want to make sure the relationship continues and we don't drift apart. Mind you, in a couple of cases I do wonder why it would matter. They're lovely people and I wish them nothing but good, but what are we getting from this succession of occasional factual updates about people I'm only loosely connected with?

My favourite people to meet up with talk about very different things. Of course we occasionally let each other know what our family and friends are up to, if there's something interesting or important to say, but mostly we end up in deep conversation and barely notice the time.

What are we talking about? I have one friend who shares my love of reading, and we'll often discuss books we've read and what we did or didn't enjoy about them. Sometimes we disagree, which only makes the conversation more interesting. I have a couple of friends – and this won't surprise you – with whom I share a fascination with what makes people tick. So we often talk about scenarios we've encountered and end up discussing why this person behaves like this, or what we could do that might help so-and-so, or how to handle a tricky client or colleague.

The thing is, the conversations I have with these friends are not only stimulating because they make us think, but by thinking aloud together we develop a far better understanding of each other. So we grow closer each time we see each other. That, in turn, means that if one of us needs emotional support, the other one will likely spot it fairly quickly and will be able to help because we know each other pretty well.

So if you want your relationships to grow closer, rather than tread water, try discussing ideas and values with your friends, rather than always just relating what your kids have been up to. You won't want – or have time – to do this with every relationship, but be aware that it's the way to deepen your friendships. Just ask what they've read lately, or what they enjoy about their job, to give the conversation an emotional and personal dimension.

> **WE GROW CLOSER EACH TIME WE SEE EACH OTHER**

RULE 63

Take it seriously

You can't beat meeting up face to face – preferably in real life, but online if you have to. Failing that, a proper phone call can really strengthen your relationship. It gives you the chance to focus properly on the way you connect with each other. Of course, that only works if you actually pay attention to the conversation.

These days, it's surprisingly hard to have a focused conversation with another person. There are lots of distractions, and phones and similar devices have to be the biggest culprits. How often have you been chatting away to someone when they start looking at their phone? However it's not only messages and emails and alerts. Sometimes your sister calls you at the same time she's cooking the family meal, or your best mate keeps looking over your shoulder at the football scores on the pub screen.

This kind of conversation is always frustrating and leaves you feeling unsatisfied. For one thing, it's simply disrespectful when the other person's attention shifts away from you. I'm not just being old-fashioned about manners here – it's that this kind of behaviour signals that you're not as important as the footie scores or the fact the vegetables are coming to the boil. That, in turn, leaves you feeling unwilling to let the conversation lead anywhere personal or emotional, because you're not confident the other person will engage with you on that level.

So if you're talking to someone you're close to – or would like to be close to – you need to give them your proper attention. Show them they're worth your time. Turn off your phone, or at least set it so that only urgent numbers can get through. Don't call them when you're doing something else, or when you're likely to be distracted. And now you have each other's attention, listen carefully to what they're saying, notice their body language, ask them questions.

Of course you can't do this every time you have a quick chat. I'm not suggesting you turn off your phone before checking with your kids what time to pick them up after club. However it's easy to get to the point where you never give people this kind of focus, even when you see them every day. You need to set aside 'proper' time with your close family and friends, when you maybe have a meal together, or go for a walk, and turn off your phones so you can focus on each other.

Similarly you need to make sure that some of your meetings with other close friends are in an atmosphere where you can both concentrate. And if you sense someone really needs to talk, you can discreetly turn off your phone, or suggest leaving the office to get a coffee, or in some other way ensure you can give the conversation your full attention.

> **SHOW THEM THEY'RE WORTH YOUR TIME**

RULE 64

Take stock

It's worth doing a mental check-up of your social life. Think about how much time you spend with other people, compared with how much time you spend in solitary activities – whether that's on social media or reading or working from home. Video gaming might fall into either category, depending on how you do it. So if you do a rough calculation, how does the result feel? Are you happy with the balance? I can't give you 'right' and 'wrong' figures because we're all different, but you should know whether the results shock you or whether it feels comfortable.

As we've already seen, the quality of your relationships will matter too. You might enjoy your own company but feel that the time you do spend with other people is largely in relationships that are really strong and important to you. That would be fine. However, if you don't like the balance once you think about it, you'll need to consider how to redress it. That's not only about spending less time in front of a screen and more time socialising. It's also about which relationships you want to put more time into, or you feel could be closer.

So consider how to get out more, or resolve to spend less time on your phone. Think about which people you'd like to be closer to, which relationships could be more meaningful, how you can focus on quality and not just quantity.

I'm going to mention animals here too. If you spend an hour a day walking the dog, you might feel reluctant to categorise that as non-social time. I completely get that. Relationships with pets can be hugely important, as countless studies have shown, and you can feel hugely connected to your dog or cat. I'm not sure how much social connection you feel with your pet hamster or stick insect,* but certainly if you have a pet you feel really close to, and

---

* That's just an example – hamster lovers please don't write in

can have a good cuddle with when you're having a bad day, that has to count for something, doesn't it?

So we'll be sensible here. If you're taking stock and your relationship with your pet is one of the most important, then obviously it counts. However that doesn't mean that human relationships aren't important too. A dog will give you unconditional love,* but it can't talk through your troubles with you and ask helpful questions you hadn't thought of.

ARE YOU HAPPY WITH THE BALANCE?

---

* A cat obviously won't, although if it chooses to love you without any sense of obligation, that's equally worth having

RULE 65

Make it better

You can always build on a good relationship to make it better. No one has the time and energy to invest in making every single social connection close and personal. However, many of us feel lonely, as we've already seen, and if that's you, the answer is to turn at least a couple of those relatively superficial friendships into something a bit deeper. A lot of friendships won't move past the initial level without a bit of effort, so put in that effort where you think it will benefit you – and don't forget the other person will gain too from having you as a closer friend.

Bear in mind that some of your current friends may already have very full lives, and maybe plenty of good strong relationships, so if they seem to resist your efforts to see more of each other don't take it personally. In any case you can develop a friendship without increasing the time you spend together – as per Rule 62, and in other ways.

Let's start with the basics. Relationships go two ways of course, so if you want others to be a good friend to you, you need to do the same for them. If you feel you'd benefit from more – or just closer – relationships, you'll need to meet people half way. Listen when they need to talk, remember their birthday, don't stand them up or let them down. You know this stuff.

If you want to develop a stronger bond with a particular person, take the initiative and move on from asking what the family are up to, or whether they'll be watching the match on Saturday. Just open up a bit and bring your emotions into the conversation. If they ask after the family, don't just tell them what the kids are up to, but confide that you're a bit worried about this, or feeling anxious about that.

If you talk about work, maybe ask their advice on how to tackle this project, or handle that colleague, or balance the demands of work with family. Ask how they deal with these things, and give them an opportunity to open up more as well. People really like to be asked for advice, and it has the double benefit of both giving you the answer and building your relationship.

Showing a bit of vulnerability opens you up and can be endearing. I'm not suggesting you start sobbing on someone's shoulder until the relationship has grown a lot further, but admitting to feeling embarrassed or hurt or nervous makes you very human, and shifts the relationship gently into one where you talk about feelings and not just facts. Over time, these little shifts enable both of you to talk more openly. You've probably worked out this is what happens unconsciously in loads of relationships, but we also have lots of friendships where we get stuck at that early superficial level. When that happens, there's no reason why you can't move things along a bit more purposefully.

> **A LOT OF FRIENDSHIPS WON'T MOVE PAST THE INITIAL LEVEL WITHOUT A BIT OF EFFORT**

RULE 66

Change your angle

One of the best ways to build great relationships is always to look at things from the other person's point of view. We all have different lives, and different personalities, and other people don't always have the same responses or priorities as us. In a good relationship it's important to understand that although we find a thing easy, someone else might find it hard. The answer may seem obvious to us, but it might not be clear to someone else. Someone's behaviour might make us angry, but it could make a different person feel hurt.

We all know people who tell us 'Here's what you should do . . .' and then proceed to tell us to do a thing that simply isn't going to work for us. Maybe we don't have it in us to be that assertive, or our family takes up too much of our time, or we're not in a position to take that kind of risk. So to avoid being that kind of person, we need to make sure we see other people's perspective. When we offer help or support or a listening ear, that will give us the empathy we need to be a better kind of friend.

I have one friend who is really open and willing to share his feelings with anyone. The only problem is, he can't see that everyone else isn't the same. So if you tell him something you consider private, he'll tell everyone. Why? Because if it was him, he wouldn't have cared if everyone knew. Another friend will complain to you at length about all her minor aches and pains, which I don't mind in the least, but our mutual friend who is seriously disabled finds quite insensitive.

Being able to understand life in someone else's shoes is an essential skill if you want to build strong relationships, as those examples show. If anyone suggests that a particular perspective or answer or piece of advice might not work for them, ask them to help you see why, rather than persisting. Better still, learn to see their point of view without having to be told. You know how you feel when someone tells you, without prompting, that they get why you feel the way you do, or they can see how hard a particular action might be for you. It's reassuring, validating, and it makes you feel that they *get* you.

So practise seeing things from other people's viewpoint. The more you do it, the more it becomes second nature. Ask yourself why this colleague struggles with a presentation you could give in your sleep, or why that friend doesn't just split with her partner if she's so unhappy. Think about what it must be like for this person who's a single dad, or that one whose elderly mother phones them at work three times a day with some minor panic. The more you think about how and why other people are different from you, the more empathetic you will become.

> **ALTHOUGH WE FIND A THING EASY, SOMEONE ELSE MIGHT FIND IT HARD**

RULE 67

Talk to strangers

I mentioned earlier that it's the deepest relationships that are most important, that you want quality and not just quantity. However I did also say, if you recall, that all the little connections add up and have value in themselves. Having a strong relationship with your partner will make you feel connected to your partner, but if you want a sense of connection with the world at large, you'll need to interact with the rest of the world too.

It's not only about a broader sense of belonging, it's also that every little bit of social contact takes you out of your own head and into the social sphere. Suppose you spend the morning doing your regular shop. When I was young, you'd call into your local fishmonger, grocer, greengrocer, butcher. They'd probably know you by name, and chat away while they were wrapping up your piece of fish, or putting oranges in a bag for you. Doing a shop was a friendly, social activity.

Nowadays, if you shop in a supermarket, you don't need to speak to anyone. You're anonymous. It might be quicker, cheaper, more efficient – or it might not – but it's certainly quite an isolated activity. It might be perfectly satisfactory, but it doesn't leave you feeling warmer, cared about, human, in the way it used to. If you have a local corner shop where they know you, you'll realise the difference.

So why not do your supermarket shop a little bit differently? Not to mention all those other anonymous activities like travelling on public transport, or walking round the park. Here's an exercise for you. Next supermarket trip, aim to interact with at least three people, above and beyond what is purely transactional. Make a positive connection, however brief.

For example, you might give some friendly reassurance to a parent looking embarrassed that their toddler is having a tantrum. Or maybe offer to reach something on a high (or low) shelf for someone who is struggling. You could joke about the best brand of beans with a customer picking a can off the shelf at the same time as you, or chat about the weather to the person behind you at the checkout. Ask the checkout assistant if they've had a long day, or wheel someone else's trolley back to the bay at the same time as yours.

Try this exercise and see if you don't feel a little bit different at the end of the process. If you did that every time you were out on your own, think how it would add to feeling like a connected part of a friendly, positive world. And that's before you consider the effect it's had on those other people you connected with. If they're having a bad day, or feeling lonely or undervalued, you might have made a real difference to them. Now doesn't that thought bring you a little bit of happiness?

> **ALL THE LITTLE CONNECTIONS ADD UP AND HAVE VALUE IN THEMSELVES**

RULE 68

Get social

Some people belong to countless clubs and groups and organisations, and make loads of friendships – of all levels. However many of us prefer not to get involved. Maybe it's just not our thing. The idea of coffee mornings or jumble sales horrifies us, we don't want to do anything sporty, we hate having to make conversation with new people.

Well, if you have all the social connection you want and need already, that's fine. But if you're one of the many people who often feel lonely, please don't dismiss this option out of hand. Let me tell you about a friend of mine who felt exactly the same way. She had a few really excellent relationships, but the kids had left home and she was spending more time on her own. She felt a social hobby might be a good idea, but she hated most organised social events, and dreaded having to make conversation with new people.

So she thought about what she really enjoyed, and a couple of things came to mind. She had worked in the theatre decades ago, so she did an internet search for local am-dram companies. Most of them didn't grab her – on what I suspect were fairly flimsy grounds – but one of them looked right up her street so on a whim she emailed them to ask if her ancient skills might be useful to them.

Anyway, she ended up joining them, and has been loving the experience. This is partly because she found an activity where she feels genuinely useful. And also because she doesn't have to make conversation with anyone – she's not there to chat, she's there to perform a function. In the course of that, of course lots of chatting goes on, but at no point does she feel under pressure to make small talk. They discuss the play they're working on, and sometimes that leads on to nattering and sometimes it doesn't.

This is a great example of how if you think it through properly there's always something that will bring you into contact with more people. My friend found an option where making small talk wasn't necessary, and where she felt she had skills that were needed. Your reservations might be very different – perhaps you need something that doesn't take too much time, or you can take a toddler along to, or where you don't have to be physically active, or where you can dip in and out depending on other demands on your time. Trust me, there will be something out there.

You can join a club, volunteer, help at the local school, work in a charity shop. It might be paid or unpaid, frequent or occasional, skilled or easy. As long as it helps you connect with more people, it will add to your total sum of happiness by giving you more social contact, and helping you to feel worthwhile. So, come on, no more sitting around thinking it's not your kind of thing. Of course it is, once you get thinking and find your own niche.

> **TRUST ME, THERE WILL BE SOMETHING OUT THERE**

RULE 69

Make friends at work

Like all the Rules in this section, some people find them so easy they're doing them already, but they're here for those who find them a bit trickier. And, mind you, also for those who are so gregarious that they have loads of relatively superficial friendships but haven't really given themselves time to develop a handful of really meaningful ones.

If you work with other people – in a shop or office or factory or studio – you're surrounded by potential friends. What's more, work is an important part of life for most of us, whether we love it, hate it, or it's just a thing we do to pay the rent. Everyone has work-related issues from time to time. You're finding the workload a bit much at the moment, your new colleague looks like they want to take over your job, your boss never seems to appreciate you, the company has changed its system for claiming travel expenses, the new software keeps glitching . . . that's life. Some little irritations, some major issues, plenty in between.

If any of your day-to-day work issues are bothering you – or any of the bigger problems that crop up from time to time – you can talk to your family and friends about it, and of course that support will help. At least up to a point. But how can your partner properly understand the knock-on frustrations of that software glitch? How can your friend really know what your boss can be like? Why would your mate recognise the pressure you're under over next month's launch?

Don't get me wrong, sometimes the distance these people have can be useful. Talking to people at one remove from your problems can really help. But wouldn't it be great *also* to have the support of friends who are living through it themselves? People you can trust not to report your remarks back to the boss, and who don't just want someone to share a bitching session with, but who genuinely want you to be happy?

It really is worth cultivating good friends at work if you possibly can. If you don't have a strong connection with anyone at work, think about who you get on well with and could develop a closer bond with. Often there are people at work who we really like, but we don't put time into socialising, or we're not sure how to build on the friendly acquaintance we've established. Well, we've covered several Rules now for strengthening friendships, so put them into practice at work.

A good relationship is always reciprocal in some way, so it's easier to connect with someone who is as ready as you to build strong connections at work, and who you can support in return. It's also easier to be friends with someone on roughly the same pay grade as you, although if things change later it doesn't have to matter. So why not invite a colleague to a social event, or for a lunchtime walk in the spring sunshine, or even ask if they fancy a drink after work so you can have a whingeing session about the new software. Take a first step towards a stronger friendship, practise the other Rules in this session, and you could discover a really rewarding new relationship.

> **IF YOU WORK WITH OTHER PEOPLE YOU'RE SURROUNDED BY POTENTIAL FRIENDS**

RULE 70

Put down roots

There's nothing for making you feel connected and happy like feeling you belong. The sense that you have a place where you fit. I grew up in London but I moved out to the West Country in my 20s and all of my children grew up here. I love the moors and the sea and the ancient woodlands and the rivers and the hills and the damp greenness of it all and, after so many years, it's where I belong.

But . . . important though my surroundings are, the reason I belong is because of the social connections I've made. I have friends and family in this part of the country now, people I recognise in the street or at the movies or doing my shopping. Countless little interactions, and more countable important ones. I still feel I have a toehold in London, and that's not because of my childhood, or the many cinemas, theatres, venues, parks, museums I enjoy visiting. No, it's because I still have family and friends there.

There's a huge satisfaction in being a part of your local community. You don't have to sit on the council or run the Chamber of Commerce. You don't have to campaign or volunteer. But listen, the people who do those things feel really rooted and incredibly tightly linked to the place they belong. It's worth taking a leaf out of their book, but find a way to do it on your terms if you don't fancy standing for election or signing petitions.

For a start, think about all the ways you're connected already. You use local shops and businesses, maybe you send your kids to local schools, or work in the area. Perhaps you contribute in other ways – volunteering, taking your old clothes to local charity shops, putting coins in a tin for local causes. The more you do – and in these examples do consciously – the more you'll encounter local people and get that sense of connection to the place *and* the people.

It might suit you better (or as well) to form links with a smaller, more manageable community. Your street, or apartment block, or village, or local park. This works really well for some people who are less gregarious, or have less time. You can meet local people if you volunteer as a gardener at the local park, or help run the toddler club on a Friday, or join the neighbourhood watch, or pick up shopping for a couple of elderly neighbours.

The thing you might notice about all of these examples is that they all involve you giving something – a bit of time or effort or thought. That's no coincidence. You'll feel a much stronger tie to your community if you give to it – in your own way – and you'll get far more back in terms of your sense of worth and feeling of belonging.

None of this is compulsory, but if you want these connections that really contribute to your happiness, find something you're able to do that will forge links with a new community, or strengthen the bonds you already have.

> **YOU'LL FEEL A MUCH STRONGER TIE TO YOUR COMMUNITY IF YOU GIVE TO IT**

HEALTH

Being healthy makes you happier. Being happy makes you healthier. Both of these statements are unsurprising, and also backed up by research. So play your cards right, and you have a win/win. This whole book is about maximising your happiness, which will benefit your health. And this section is all about how to be healthier in ways that will boost your enjoyment of life.

Of course you don't have control over every aspect of your health, and anything can arrive out of the blue from a common cold to something more serious. However there's a great deal that you can influence. If you make the healthiest choices where you can, you'll maximise your chances of staying as healthy as possible for as long as possible. The chances of illness – major or minor – will be lessened, and your body will be in the best state to cope with any ailments and illnesses that might come your way.

It's clearly a good thing to meet any kind of ill health in the most positive mental and physical state you can. But of course you don't have to wait until you're unwell to get the benefits. If you follow these next few Rules, not only will you have the best chance of remaining in good health, you'll also be able to get the most out of your life. If you can wake up every morning feeling well rested and full of energy, it will be so much easier to seize the day.

RULE 71

Get some sleep

Let's look at the real basics for being healthy. You're never going to feel your best unless you have a good night's sleep, as often as you can. Your body repairs itself when you sleep, from healing wounds to stress recovery, and a decent night's sleep is good for your brain and your cognitive functioning too. In fact it's good for all your major bodily systems, from the heart and circulation to your muscles and your digestion.

So it's essential, if you want to be as healthy as possible, that your normal routine allows for a good night's sleep. For most adults, that's between about seven and nine hours a night. Of course there will be the occasional night when you're out late, or you just can't drop off. The important thing is to be able to get about eight hours' sleep in a typical night.

Logically, that means you need to go to sleep about eight hours before you get up – look, this isn't rocket science. But many people make this impossible for themselves. Suppose you have to be up at 7am. Well, if you aren't lying in bed with the lights out by 11pm, it's not going to happen, is it? It's your choice, but if you want to be healthier – and happier – you need to organise your life so you can do this.

What's more, if you go straight from doing something very stimulating – mentally or physically – straight into bed, it will most likely take you longer to get to sleep. So aim for at least half an hour before sleep time when you wind down in some way. Low lights, gentle music, meditation, a hot bath, whatever works for you. That way, when you get into bed and turn out the light, sleep will come much more readily.

Most of us will go through phases of insomnia at some time in our lives – extended periods when we struggle either to get to sleep, or to stay asleep, and as a result don't clock up the hours of sleep we need to feel healthy. For some people this is a long-term chronic problem, while many of us experience it for a few weeks or months for all sorts of reasons such as pain, stress, excitement, menopause, grief, medication, poor mental health, alcohol consumption.

The real takeaway from this Rule is that insomnia affects your sleep, and that has knock-on effects on your life in general, your happiness and your mental health. And that means that you need to do something about it. Don't just wait for it to go away. If you have an idea what's behind it, you may be able to address it yourself. Or you can research ways to overcome it. Following most of the other Rules in this section should help you too. And if all that still doesn't do the trick, see your doctor. They should be able to help or to refer you. Importantly, don't just live with it. Do something about it.

YOU'RE NEVER GOING TO FEEL YOUR BEST UNLESS YOU HAVE A GOOD NIGHT'S SLEEP

RULE 72

Enjoy the fresh air

Now you're getting a good night's sleep, the next priority is the air you breathe. Fresh air is good for your immune system, your lungs, your energy levels, your mental health – to name but a few. If you can spend just 20 minutes a day outside, it will really help your health and your happiness.

If you're lucky enough to live near the countryside, so much the better, but even in a city it makes a big difference to go to a park or open space if you can. It's further from traffic pollution, and being around green spaces – whether that's a park or your own garden – has been shown to boost people's mood. If you can get out of the city altogether, that's even better.

Breathing in fresh air is the aim, and all you have to do is walk, exercise or focus on your breathing to make sure your lungs suck in as much of it as possible. It will help you to sleep, it boosts your immune system, and all that oxygen gives you energy and helps your brain to function.

Better still – and I appreciate you have limited control over this – is to get outside when it's sunny. You can't turn the sun on and off, but if the day is changeable, try to get outside during the sunshine for all sorts of extra benefits. Sunshine enables your body to make its own vitamin D, which is good for your bones and muscles, and for your immune system. It also increases your brain's production of serotonin, one of the hormones that makes you feel calm and helps your brain to focus.

Interestingly, we make the most vitamin D during the first few minutes out in the sunshine, so you don't need to spend long periods outside to get the benefit. In any case you might need to be careful not to let your skin burn, or you'll do more harm than good. It does help to expose more of your skin for those few minutes though, so roll up your sleeves, wear shorts, or otherwise give yourself the most benefit.

Fresh air and sunshine. It's a pretty traditional recipe for good health that our grandparents would have recognised, and it's backed up by more modern science. This health lark's not so difficult, is it? A lot of it is just common sense, but it can easily get lost in the hurly-burly of life if we don't make a conscious effort to give it the priority it deserves. So build it into your routine in some way. Ten minutes in the garden or on the balcony with a cup of tea first thing in the morning, or when you get home. Or maybe get into the habit of taking 20 minutes for lunch in the park every day. Even walking the dog during the day rather than after dark is a plus.

> **FRESH AIR AND SUNSHINE. IT'S A PRETTY TRADITIONAL RECIPE FOR GOOD HEALTH**

RULE 73

Get moving

Inactivity is the enemy of good health. Our bodies are designed to be on the go much of the time, and if you live a modern, largely sedentary lifestyle it's not good for you. I'm not talking about specific exercise (yet). This is about sitting at a desk for most of the day, or indeed on a sofa or in front of a screen. Sitting too long slows your metabolism, which is bad for your weight and your blood pressure, and weakens your muscles and bones, among other things.

I'm not telling you anything you don't know already. But what are you going to do about it? It's not easy if your job requires you to sit all day, or your favourite pastimes involve sitting in front of a computer or a sewing machine or a steering wheel. However being healthier is good in itself, as well as feeding into your general wellbeing, so it's important you find a way to counteract your inactive lifestyle.

What you need are strategies that will give you a reason to stand up and move around regularly – at least every hour, and ideally more than that. I've worked from home for years, sitting at a desk, and that makes it a bit easier because there are plenty of hacks for making me move about. For example, I always put a laundry wash through during work time, because it gives me a reason to stand up and put it on, stand up about an hour later to hang things up and put the tumble dryer on, and again to empty the dryer. I don't have that motivation every day though (not since I stopped doing the kids' laundry). If you're at home, you can sometimes do a similar thing with cooking.

If you work in an office, you can make yourself a rule that you go to colleagues' desks if you need to speak to them, rather than always message or email. You can also make yourself a coffee or tea every hour (maybe decaf coffee if you're going to drink it that frequently) – and have a stretch or a walk around at the same time.

I aim to stand up and walk around when I'm on the phone, which happens a lot some days and not at all others. It's a useful habit to get into though, at home or at work. I know people who get on well with standing desks too – it's still good to move around, but certainly healthier to be standing all day than sitting.

If you're watching old-fashioned TV you can make a point of moving during the ad breaks – let the dog out, do the washing up, water the houseplants. You were going to do all those things anyway, and it's much better to intersperse them than to get them all done at once and then sit in front of the TV for hours without moving.

The more of these strategies you can use the better, along with any others you can think of. You can set a regular alarm to remind you every 30 minutes or so, because half the problem is you get immersed in something and don't notice you've been immobile for the last three hours. We'll look at regular exercise separately, but here the important thing is never to sit down for too long.

> **WHAT YOU NEED ARE STRATEGIES THAT WILL GIVE YOU A REASON TO STAND UP AND MOVE AROUND REGULARLY**

RULE 74

Exercise more

If you're a regular sports person, or run several times a week, or visit the gym frequently, or otherwise keep very active, you won't need this Rule. Well done. For the rest of us, perhaps a bit more exercise would be a good thing. Now listen, I dislike formal exercise as much as anyone – I only wish I could enjoy it, but school pretty much guaranteed my lifelong aversion to it. However, that doesn't mean I can't get plenty of good exercise. It just means I have to find other ways to do it. No one has to cycle ten miles a day, or lift weights, or play hockey, if they don't want to.

As with moving about more if you have a sedentary job, this is all about putting in the effort to find those strategies that will become effortless once they're habit. When I worked in central London, I always took the stairs up to the street from the Tube, rather than the escalator – or if necessary I walked up the escalator. Similarly when I worked on the second floor of a building. These things quickly become so automatic you don't think about them.

Of course, taking the stairs alone won't be enough, but enough hacks like this add up to a pretty active lifestyle. Get off the bus or train a stop or two early, park five or ten minutes' walk from where you're going, go on foot instead of taking the bus or the car. Walking is really good for you, and if you can fit a regular walk into your day – with or without a dog – you're a long way towards keeping healthy on the exercise front.

My mother's generation stayed pretty active and fit, and hardly any of them ran marathons or went to the gym. They just walked everywhere and kept active. They didn't have the temptation of TVs and computers, and a lot of housework and chores were more demanding, and that was good enough for their health. It shows that you don't have to do formal 'exercise' if you don't want to, so long as you stay physically busy in other ways.

There are loads of activities that keep you active without that being the point of them. Without even leaving the house, DIY or gardening can keep you active and sometimes give you a good workout. Dancing too – you don't have to go out specially, you can just put on a favourite track. There are plenty of leisure activities that give you good exercise too, without having to join the football team. You're looking for about 20 minutes a day of moderate exercise, so it shouldn't be too hard to achieve.

The important thing is to start small and build up, so you don't scare yourself off. Just create a new habit here or there, and once they're established maybe add another. Think about things you enjoy that happen to be physically a bit more demanding, and see what you can incorporate regularly into your life. Not only can exercise make you feel good in itself, you also get the benefit of being healthier and fitter.

> **NO ONE HAS TO CYCLE TEN MILES A DAY, OR LIFT WEIGHTS, OR PLAY HOCKEY, IF THEY DON'T WANT TO**

RULE 75

Manage your energy

It's natural that our energy ebbs and flows throughout the day. That's true not only of humans but of many other animals too, as you'll know if you have a dog or a cat. So it's not a thing that we need to eliminate, but we will be happier if we work with it rather than against it. In order to do that, you have to learn how your own system works.

As kids, it's instilled in us that we have to get up at this time, go to school at that time, do maths here and sport there, without any say in whether it's working for us. So as adults, we're already programmed to follow a schedule without thought for whether it's actually the most productive or fulfilling way to function. However, while your boss might not look kindly on you turning up at lunchtime because it fits your personal rhythms better, there are lots of things you can do to manage your energy better.

The most important of these is to recognise that your energy fluctuates, and your mental and physical energy levels aren't always in sync, and that's normal. The sensible approach is to work with it, not to fight it. Having accepted that, the next thing is to begin to learn your own patterns. Generally speaking they'll be fairly consistent, unless something has changed. For example they might be thrown out by a bad night's sleep, or an unusually strenuous day, but otherwise they'll be largely predictable. They'll change over time too, in response to having children, or ageing, or menopause, or illness, so be aware that just because you were at your most productive at 2 am in your teens, doesn't necessarily mean you still are.

Other things will affect your energy too, such as vigorous exercise, or low fluid levels, or coffee, or meals – indeed maybe certain foods in particular. So learn to recognise that you're likely to go through a period of low or high energy after these. Some may reduce your physical energy but increase your mental acuity, for example.

Once you have this information, you can organise your day much more productively, and avoid the lows that your system might otherwise experience – for example if you consume something sugary after physical exercise, or try to focus your mind on figures after a poor night's sleep.

Research shows that people who vary their routines are typically happier than those who don't, so shuffling activities around to fit your energy levels can be actively helpful. If your energy starts to drop, you'll know whether you need to drink some water, or take an after-lunch nap, or deal with some easy task at work, or get out for five minutes of fresh air.

The more you are in control of managing your energy, the better. Move tasks around, or switch up your routines – at work and at home – so that you make the most of them. You'll have the satisfaction of being more productive, and you'll avoid the low mood that comes from trying to fight the system.

> **YOUR ENERGY FLUCTUATES, AND YOUR MENTAL AND PHYSICAL ENERGY LEVELS AREN'T ALWAYS IN SYNC**

RULE 76

Eat well

As I said before, a lot of staying healthy is stuff you already know. The problem – for many of us – is actually doing it. But as well as trying to keep to a healthy weight, the quality of the food we eat is important. Just because your weight might not be worrying your doctor, that doesn't mean your diet is necessarily good for you. If you want to be as healthy as possible, and as happy, you need to be eating foods that are nutritious, and which don't give you mood swings or make you feel low.

I'm fairly sceptical about a lot of diets – whether for weight loss or for nutrition. In my experience the results rarely last because most diets are too prescriptive to be sustainable. Not only does this mean that they don't work in the long term, it also leaves you feeling frustrated and perhaps even a bit of a failure when you struggle to stick to them after the first few weeks.

So this Rule is about finding a way to eat more healthily that you can sustain permanently. That doesn't mean you never have a day off, and it doesn't mean anything has to be entirely off the table,* so long as you mostly stick to it most of the time. That's way better than sticking religiously to a diet for a couple of months and then giving up on it.

You've got the rest of your life for this, so if it takes a while to gradually incorporate better habits into your regime, that's OK. Take it at a speed that you can cope with, so long as you keep adapting until you arrive at a healthy and sustainable diet. There are two things you're trying to achieve here – eating more of the healthy foods, and eating fewer unhealthy foods. Look, you know what those are. It's not that you didn't realise sugar was bad for you, or vegetables are good. So the challenge is to work out why you aren't eating as healthily as you could, and do something about it.

---

* Apologies

Is it difficult to find healthy food for your work lunch? Are you too tired to cook when you get home? Do your mates always want to go for pizza? If you put your mind to it, you can find ways round all of these – such as taking your own lunch in to work, or batch cooking at weekends.

Listen, it's up to you. You can keep coming up with excuses if you like. It's not my problem if you insist on being unhealthy. Or you can take responsibility for your own life, your own health, your own happiness, and do something about it. Just lay off the fad diets and address the underlying reasons you don't eat as well as you could. Improve what you need to – feed the changes in gradually* so it doesn't feel like a big deal. Then stick to it most of the time, and don't beat yourself up over the odd day it all goes to pot.

> **THE CHALLENGE IS TO WORK OUT WHY YOU AREN'T EATING AS HEALTHILY AS YOU COULD, AND DO SOMETHING ABOUT IT**

---

* Apologies again

RULE 77

Drink well

It's no good taking proper care of what you eat, and then drinking what and when you please. Knowing how to drink is a bit more nuanced – there are some obvious rules, but a lot of hazy advice in between. So a big part of getting your liquid intake right is about monitoring yourself and being aware of the effect your drinking has on you.

Clearly alcohol is one part of this. We all know that too much alcohol is a Bad Thing. Having said that, getting a bit tipsy once in a while isn't the end of the world, and there's increasing evidence that certain alcoholic drinks, such as red wine, are good for you in moderation. The most important principle is that you should be in charge, and not the drink.

You should always feel perfectly able to say no to a drink, whether that's a few days' abstinence a month, or a last drink on an evening out. The time to worry is when you feel unable to resist. If this is starting to happen, you have a problem and you need to address it now – with help if necessary – before it gets out of hand. Be honest with yourself, and maybe practise saying no from time to time if there's a chance it might be harder than you want to believe.

That's alcohol, but how about other drinks? You need to keep an eye on the reliable science reports here, because new studies are coming out all the time that shift the goalposts. For example, it's certainly a good idea to drink plenty of water, but the two litres a day rule turns out to be pretty random. You can drink too much water, and one pretty good way to judge your intake is that you should typically need to pee more than five times a day, but less than about ten.

What's more important is how you feel, and how to use water to boost your energy or to prevent lows. This all ties in with how you eat, and how you manage your energy through the day. Your body should be telling you when you need to drink, or when you've drunk enough, so learn the signals. Maybe water is especially helpful when you hit a drop in mood, or before you eat – we're all different so you need to understand your own body and your own moods.

The same goes for coffee, which can be a useful energy boost, and has health benefits, but is easy to become reliant on. Maybe experiment with decaf, at least after the first two or three cups of the day. Tea – especially green tea – can really boost your mood as well as your energy, so learn to understand how your body interacts with that too. And energy drinks or artificially sweetened drinks can have their downsides, so again know your own reactions and use them to your advantage.

It's surprising just how much influence our liquid intake, of all kinds, can have on our mood and our overall wellbeing. So it makes sense to monitor it for a while until you understand how to get the most from it, and avoid the negative effects on your health or your emotions.

THE MOST IMPORTANT PRINCIPLE IS THAT YOU SHOULD BE IN CHARGE, AND NOT THE DRINK

RULE 78

Don't poison yourself

This is a bit of a bonkers Rule to need, but most of us ignore it to some degree. The last couple of Rules had some good examples of this, and illustrate how even the most innocuous seeming substances can potentially be toxic. Even water, if you drink it in excessive quantities. So this Rule is as much about not consuming too much of things – to the point where they become toxic – as it is about saying no altogether.

Some people might argue that this moderation is even acceptable for some recreational drugs at the milder end of the spectrum, and there are cultures around the world that consume some drugs which are banned elsewhere. Of course, there are also many drugs which are just a no-no. Remember, this is all about your overall happiness – not just a few minutes' high – and there are substances which are absolutely not worth experimenting with, given the risks to your long-term health. In particular anything that can quickly become addictive, not least because it takes control and agency away from you, which is not going to make you happy.

For some people, it's prescription drugs that are a problem. There's a reason why you can only get them on prescription. I'm absolutely not advocating giving them up unilaterally, but if the side-effects are affecting your moods or your health, talk to your GP seriously about ways to mitigate this, or reduce certain dosages.

This Rule isn't just about drugs and alcohol though. Again, you need to listen to your own body and keep an eye on *everything* you put into it. Clearly tobacco is on this list, along with other forms of smoking such as vapes. I spent about 50 years trying to give up smoking* before successfully stopping. So if you don't smoke, don't start. You might think it looks cool and grown-up, but it really isn't. If you already smoke, you don't need me to tell you

---

* I started when I was five, believe it or not

it isn't making you happy or healthy – or rich – so don't give up on quitting. God knows it's hard, but it is possible. Even after 50 years of committed smoking. The trick is to find a strong enough motivation, and that isn't easy. It's no good just wanting to want to. You have to *really* want to.

And then there are all the other things we consume that we know are bad for us. Refined sugar, processed food, caffeine . . . you don't have to turn into a rainbow-clad, sandal-wearing, vegan, knit-your-own-pasta hippie.* The aim isn't to turn into someone you're not, doing things that don't work for you. It's just a matter of recognising the choices that don't actually make you feel healthy and happy, and not making them. Or at least not making them too often.

> YOU DON'T HAVE TO TURN INTO A RAINBOW-CLAD, SANDAL-WEARING, VEGAN, KNIT-YOUR-OWN-PASTA HIPPIE

---

* I knew lots of those when I lived in Glastonbury, some of whom were lovely, but it's a whole lifestyle choice

RULE 79

Build your resistance

The best way to be healthy is to avoid getting ill in the first place. Failing that, you want to recover as quickly as possible when you do become unwell. In both cases, the crucial factor that you have control over is your immune system. The better condition you can keep that in, the better your system will cope with – or ideally sidestep – any illness.

Of course this applies to coping with everyday colds and bugs, and also with anything more significant, from disease to recovering from surgery. However a strong immune system will help you feel good every day, and boost your energy, your mood, and your ability to bounce back from everyday setbacks. So you need to know how to get your immune system functioning as well as possible.

If you're prone to coming down with bugs and infections, if you feel tired all the time, if any cuts and grazes take longer than you'd expect to heal, if you're developing allergies, or your eczema is flaring, or you're starting to get headaches, these can all be signs that your immune system isn't as robust as it could be. Of course check with your GP if any of these symptoms are persistent or worry you, but whatever the cause, a strong immune system can only help. The good news is that many of the Rules we've already covered will make a big difference.

Eating and drinking well, good sleep, exercise, and fresh air – including vitamin D – all help to strengthen your system overall. For example, when you sleep your body produces proteins that help to ward off infections, so reduced or interrupted nights will interfere with this. Not that you should worry about the odd unsatisfactory night, but it's yet another reason to organise your schedule so that your normal routine allows time for a good night's sleep.

Drinking plenty of water is now known to play a significant part in strengthening your immune system, so it really does help if you can make sure you stay properly hydrated throughout the day. You want to maintain a steady level of hydration so drink frequently, don't restrict it to meal times, for instance.

Your immune system doesn't like stress, so if your lifestyle is highly stressed, it's well worth looking for manageable changes to reduce the stress levels for the sake of your overall health. That could mean reducing the stress in some way – cutting your hours, reducing your commute, finding help and support – or it might be a case of managing the stress better, such as exercise or meditation or more short breaks or a daily walk.

This Rule essentially reinforces the last few, in reminding you of why they're important in so many ways, in terms of boosting your overall mood and your ability to enjoy life.

> **THE BEST WAY TO BE HEALTHY IS TO AVOID GETTING ILL IN THE FIRST PLACE**

RULE 80

Think long term

We've covered several Rules for improving – or sustaining – your health, all of which will feed into your moods as well. So they'll make you feel better in themselves, and they'll give you the best chance of avoiding pain and illness. But listen, if you need to make significant changes here, you don't have to do it all at once.

You have years, decades, ahead of you, so if it takes a few months to get into healthy routines that's really not a big deal. As with changing your eating habits, it's much better to take it slow and steady. The risk otherwise is that it will be too complicated to make loads of changes at once, and you'll hurl yourself at it with enthusiasm and then run out of steam when it doesn't immediately fit into your life. Then in a few months' time this book will be gathering dust on a shelf, or kicked under the sofa, and you'll be back to your less-than-ideal ways.

Think about the small changes that will make the most difference for you, and just focus on those. That might be going to bed earlier so you regularly get a decent night's sleep, or cutting down on caffeine by switching to decaf after lunchtime. Introduce one thing at a time, and get it properly embedded before you move on to the next.

About 25 years ago I went on some fad diet – before I gave it up. It required me to stop putting sugar in my tea. Needless to say the diet fizzled out with no discernible long-lasting effects, except that 25 years on I still don't take sugar in my tea. I now realise I should just have focused on that and not bothered with the rest of the diet.

I was talking to someone the other day who told me she gave up chocolate a year ago and hasn't touched it since. She found it addictive and reckoned she needed to go cold turkey. That was the only change she made, and it worked for her in the most important way – which is that 12 months on she's stuck to it. So you see, these little changes are much easier to sustain, and you can keep dropping in new ones as and when the previous one is established.

Meantime, start monitoring your energy and your moods. Observe whether there are certain times or occasions when you feel a bit flat, or begin to flag. Do they correlate with what you've been doing or consuming? Do they typically happen at the same time every day? Are they affected by how much sleep you've had, or how much exercise you've done? This will give you the best clue as to which adjustments to make next. Not only that, but if you can make changes that help with those moments when you flag, you'll see the benefit quickly and that will motivate you to stick with them. If you look back you'll likely find that you've made loads of changes over the years that have stuck. They may not always have been for the better, and they may not have been conscious, but it shows that you are perfectly capable of long-term changes.

> **INTRODUCE ONE THING AT A TIME, AND GET IT PROPERLY EMBEDDED BEFORE YOU MOVE ON TO THE NEXT**

CURIOSITY

Being curious about the world around you is vital from an evolutionary perspective. We adapted to be curious so that we could search for food and shelter, and test out potential dangers. That's not exclusive to humans of course, but it's very human to explore things we don't actually need to understand, from ideas and language to new places and people.

Studies have shown that people who are inquisitive, who explore their world, report more positive emotions and lower levels of anxiety, greater wellbeing and more life satisfaction. It's not yet established that curiosity causes good feelings (it could be that happy people are more curious) but it looks likely that it goes both ways, and makes sense that some of the effects of curiosity would be positive. Some research has focused on work and concluded that being curious gives you a greater enjoyment of your work, and makes you less prone to stress and burnout.

Sounds like a wonder drug doesn't it? And in a way it is. It seems that when we satisfy those curious urges, our bodies generate a hit of dopamine, one of the hormones connected with feelings of pleasure. So it makes sense that we should do our best to explore and investigate, to ask questions and seek out information, in order to cultivate our sense of curiosity.

Babies and children are insatiably curious, constantly seeking to understand the world around them. Over time, as we feel we know the essentials, it's easy to sink into a comfortable adulthood where we stick to our comfort zones and don't need to explore. However, just because we don't need to do it, doesn't mean it wouldn't be a positive experience if we just tried it. So take a look at the next few Rules, and see if you can't find new ways to look at your world, and improve your life in the process.

RULE 81

The journey is more important than the destination

OK, you're going to be more inquisitive, more enquiring, ask more questions, seek out new experiences. That's great, and it's going to improve your life in all kinds of ways. It seems that people who look for new experiences, and investigate ideas, create a rich environment for learning and developing. This may well explain the correlation that researchers have found between people who are curious, and those who are intelligent and good at solving problems. As always, the fact there's a correlation doesn't prove which is causing which, but it seems likely they feed each other.

So being more inquisitive, seeking out ideas and experiences and information, can make you smarter. Seems pretty plausible to me. And look at what I just said – being inquisitive, looking for knowledge, exploring ideas. None of those are about answers. Yes, of course you will often find answers, and that can be very satisfying, but it's really about the process. You don't stretch your mind when someone gives you information on a plate. The stimulation comes from searching it out for yourself.

It's true that in the short term there may be a dopamine hit from arriving at a conclusion, from reaching a destination, whether it's literal or metaphorical. But that doesn't mean there's no enjoyment in the route you take to get there. And it also means that the exercise is worthwhile even when there is no destination, or not one that you ever reach.

One of my children announced at the age of about three that when he grew up, he was going to know everything there was to know. So far he hasn't succeeded, but he's had a lot of fun trying. The thing is, the more you learn, the more you realise there is to learn. As Tennyson* wrote, 'All experience is an arch wherethrough gleams that untravelled world, whose margin fades forever and forever when I move.'

Good answers tend to open up fresh questions, so there's no point being fixated on an end point. As with the best holidays, what you want to do is to enjoy the journey. Take the scenic route, not the shortcut, and explore all the intriguing looking byways and detours. There's nothing wrong with arriving at a destination, but it's not essential, and there's no need to rush it. Of course you sometimes just need a quick answer, but learn to savour the search when you have the opportunity.

> BEING INQUISITIVE, LOOKING FOR KNOWLEDGE, EXPLORING IDEAS – NONE OF THOSE ARE ABOUT ANSWERS

---

* I'm allowed to quote him without upsetting my publisher, because he died over 130 years ago. And no one has expressed the point better since then. If you're curious to know where the line comes from, the poem is called *Ulysses*

RULE 82

Ask yourself questions

If you're going to become more curious about the world – and however naturally inquisitive you already are, the more the better – there's no better place to start than the inside of your own head. I hope that as a Rules Player this is something you're getting used to anyway. But really, getting to know what makes you the person you are is vital to your happiness in general, as well as being the perfect starting point for your curiosity. Understanding your own internal landscape is an unending journey, but every new thing you learn will be both fascinating and useful.

So be curious. When you notice yourself feeling anxious or stressed or excited or confused, ask yourself why. Not to judge or criticise yourself, but simply out of curiosity. And remember the last Rule, which means you're not looking for quick, pat answers – 'because this is stressful', 'because it's exciting' – but really trying to get to the bottom of what makes it so. Especially where not everyone necessarily feels as you do, so your feelings aren't universal. It's likely that near enough everyone would feel scared when being charged by an angry lion, but not everyone gets anxious before a meeting, or feels excited at the prospect of reorganising their desk. So why do you?

It might be down to your past, or your genetic make-up, or your previous experience of meetings.* It might be because of the way you view the exercise. Let me give you an example. I know many people who feel daunted by the prospect of reorganising their desk, or their kitchen, or their garage. And I know plenty who feel quite excited by it. Everyone is different, but typically those who feel daunted are focused on the process, and those who feel excited are focused on the outcome – a tidy, well-organised space.

Now in this instance, questioning yourself, and recognising that you're daunted because you're thinking about the process, is not

---

* Or indeed of being charged by an angry lion

only interesting in itself, but could also be very helpful. And of course you can take it further – why are you the kind of person who is daunted by the process, rather than someone who is enjoying the anticipation of the end result?

The better you understand yourself, the better you can equip yourself to cope with life. And if you want to change behaviours that aren't benefiting you, you'll need to find explanations for them first. Not to mention satisfying your curiosity about how you tick, and exploring which people and experiences have shaped you over the years.

> **UNDERSTANDING YOUR OWN INTERNAL LANDSCAPE IS AN UNENDING JOURNEY**

RULE 83

Be inquisitive about people

No, don't ask them overly personal questions. But do ask them questions. Other people are endlessly fascinating – I would say that – and indeed I have said it elsewhere. Connecting with people is important in itself, as we know, but it's also valuable to be curious about them.

Asking questions is always a great place to start in a conversation, both with new people and with old friends. It shows you're interested in the other person and, assuming you listen properly to the answers, that will make them feel good. You'll probably start with relatively superficial, polite questions talking to someone you barely know, but you can ask your close friends more in-depth questions, once you know which raw spots to avoid, or simply notice what you'd really like to know about them.

Factual questions are fine, and generally safe – 'where do you live?' or 'what do you do for a living?' – but things get really interesting when you can ask people about how they think, what they believe, what drives them. Your curiosity can bring you close and make the friendship deeper, and it helps us to understand people too. Both the person you're talking with, and people more broadly.

When I was in my 20s, I had a very close friend who attempted suicide. Fortunately she didn't succeed, and I visited her in hospital. She had a young baby at the time, and I'd never understood how people could take their own lives when it meant leaving young children behind. So I asked her about what went on in her head in that regard. Her answer not only told me more about her, but gave me a real insight into how many people think in that situation, and ensured I'd never again be judgemental about it. It's one of the reasons I went on to volunteer as a Samaritan for several years.

The more personal the questions, the more interesting the answers can be, so obviously you need to be careful not to be too intrusive. But asking people questions about their thoughts and feelings and beliefs tends to elicit much more interesting answers than just enquiring after facts. Having said that, even the most basic conversations can give you information, and it's an interesting exercise to consider what you've learnt about someone you've just chatted to for five minutes.

Even a chat with a stranger at a checkout can give away a great deal in terms of the vibe they give off – do they come across as chilled or anxious, health conscious, house proud, in a hurry, family-orientated? It's interesting after this kind of brief conversation to reflect on all the things you've learnt – or had reason to suspect – that weren't actually said.

> **THE MORE PERSONAL THE QUESTIONS, THE MORE INTERESTING THE ANSWERS CAN BE**

RULE 84

Understand conflict

When it comes to disagreeing or falling out with people, curiosity can be your lifeline. The key to resolving most conflicts, large or small, is being able to see the other person's perspective. So if you find yourself getting into an argument with a colleague, or you and your partner are edging towards a row, or a neighbour dispute is starting to turn nasty, now is the time to stop arguing and start asking yourself why they feel the way they do.

Imagine yourself in the other person's shoes, and think about why this matters to them enough to fight over it. They're probably not enjoying this any more than you are, so what drives them to think it's worth falling out over? Almost no one actively seeks out this kind of conflict, so they must have strong reasons for adopting their position. So it can only help if you explore what those reasons might be.

Suppose your neighbour is upset because you planted a fast-growing climber on your side of the boundary fence. It's on your side, so it's none of their business what you choose to plant, right? That's technically true, so why have they chosen to pick a fight with you over it? Imagine yourself in their garden – what difference is it making to them? Perhaps it keeps sending up suckers on their side of the fence, and they don't have the time or the expertise to deal with them. Maybe it's choking and killing off the tree they planted to commemorate their mother when she died.

Of course, the best way to find out the reason is to ask. It's a great rule in any ongoing dispute, or a one-off discussion that's becoming heated. If you catch yourself feeling defensive, or the other person becoming emotional, ask a question. It makes it harder for you to feel angry, and it gives them the chance to feel heard, and to see that you want to understand their perspective.

Obviously passive-aggressive questions are not the way to go here. You need to ask genuinely curious questions. Ask them to explain something to you, ask them what they need, ask them what their parameters would be for a satisfactory outcome. Politely get them to show you their perspective. It's by far the most effective way to de-escalate any kind of conflict, not least because it shows that you want to find a solution that works for them as well as for you.

But it's not just about making them feel their viewpoint matters. Once you can see what they need, it's much easier to find a resolution that works for you both. Maybe your colleague really doesn't want to take risks because they can't afford another failure in the boss's eyes, perhaps your neighbour has a shady garden and really doesn't want to lose their one sunny spot. Once you understand, you can empathise – regardless of your conflicting needs – and that will help you to stop fighting, and start putting your heads together to come up with an answer that works for you both, even if it entails a bit of compromise.

> **ONCE YOU UNDERSTAND, YOU CAN EMPATHISE**

RULE 85

Take a deep dive

When I was starting out as a writer, I used to freelance putting together press releases for local companies, among other things. One day my contact at the local council called me up to say please could I write them a press release as they'd just taken delivery of a brand new, state-of-the-art, rear-end compactor–loader vehicle. I paused for a moment and then asked if they meant a dust cart? Indeed they did, and I agreed to come and meet their vehicle and write their press release.

The thing that stays with me about this, other than the entertainingly euphemistic terminology, was that I assumed this would be a fairly uninspiring job – although work was work and I wasn't going to turn it down. But the more I learnt about this machine, and the challenges of waste disposal, the more interesting it became. It only occupied about a day of my life, but for that day I was fascinated by dust carts.

The fact is that pretty much anything is interesting if you look deep enough. On that occasion I was being paid to be curious, but it would have been interesting regardless. The more inquisitive you become, the more questions you ask, the more surprised you are by how many things are genuinely intriguing to know about. I've had plenty of conversations with people whose job initially sounded quite dull, but turned out to be anything but once I got them talking about it. I'm thinking of supermarket cashiers, for example, typeface designers, project managers, air-conditioning engineers, removals drivers. Almost anyone to be honest, if you can find the right questions to ask.

The incurious tend to write things off as being boring or uninteresting without giving them a chance. However if you want to expand your knowledge, learn new things, find the joy in exploration and discovery, you need to approach everything with the attitude that it might be really interesting. Of course you won't want to take a deep dive into everything – no one has time for that – but you can still recognise that anything might be interesting if you had the time, rather than assuming it won't be. And when you do get the chance – whether you're chatting to someone new or writing a press release – approach it in the belief that there's something interesting there if you can just find it. That will inspire you to ask the right questions, genuinely to search for the nuggets that will interest you.

Of course we all have topics we naturally find interesting, and others that have never grabbed us. I'm not saying you have to go and study football or insurance or computer science in depth if you just aren't inspired by those subjects. But recognise that they aren't boring in themselves, even if you don't really get them, and if you're stuck talking to an insurance broker at a party don't assume they'll have nothing interesting to say. Meanwhile, when it comes to new topics you haven't formed much of an opinion about yet, always give them a chance.

> **PRETTY MUCH ANYTHING IS INTERESTING IF YOU LOOK DEEP ENOUGH**

RULE 86

Look for adventure

Imagine the experience of white water rafting in the tropics – wouldn't you like to know how that feels? Or how about a trip to Italy to see all that incredible art and architecture? Or maybe a wildlife safari in Africa or Canada? Holidays like these would indeed be inspiring and stimulating, but most of us can't afford them, at least not more than once in a lifetime.

If you're naturally curious, and seek out new experiences, of course you'd love to take this kind of trip. You'd meet new people, broaden your understanding of the world, try new things. But you can still achieve those things on a more modest scale if you adopt that same spirit of adventure 52 weeks a year. The scale isn't important – it's the mindset that matters.

The thing about these holidays is that it's quite possible to spend most of your year doing the same old, same old, and save all your excitement for the one fortnight you go abroad. But how much better to look for little adventures every day. That will stretch you far more, and stimulate your curiosity far better, with all the associated benefits we've seen. And without breaking the bank.

I live in a part of the UK's West Country which is known for its countless tiny twisty interconnecting lanes. They're like a random spider's web and notoriously easy to get lost in. One of my local friends makes a point of exploring a lane they've never been down before at least once a week, just to see where it goes. Sometimes it takes them to a stunning view, other times they discover a handy shortcut, or a useful farm shop, or they spot a kingfisher or a heron. This is free adventure, and always fun.

Another friend of mine has become a passionate member of a local choir, all because she was invited along for moral support by a friend looking for a new outlet after their partner died. My friend wasn't keen at all – assumed she wouldn't enjoy it – and only went along out of a desire to be encouraging. She supposed it would be a bit of an adventure for an evening, and it's turned into a whole new chapter.

If you live in a city, you're likely to be spoilt for choice when it comes to buying food – ingredients or cafés or takeaways or restaurants. So experiment. Try something new. And investigate why a particular food goes with a particular culture, how it fits into their cuisine, where and how it grows, what flavours it's traditionally combined with.

If you can afford to travel the world collecting experiences and learning about different cultures, that's great. Be curious about the places you visit – don't spend your whole time lying on a beach or lazing in the hotel pool. Even if you've gone for a rest you can sample the food and chat to the locals, go for a walk and visit a nearby landmark. But if you can't afford it, there are plenty of other ways to exercise your curiosity without leaving home. You might just need to leave your comfort zone is all.

> **THE SCALE ISN'T IMPORTANT – IT'S THE MINDSET THAT MATTERS**

RULE 87

Love a rabbit hole

I have a very simple way to tell which of my friends have a curious nature and which don't. These days, knowledge is at our fingertips any time we like, so long as we have a phone or a tablet or a PC nearby. So pretty much always. And yet I know lots of people who will say 'I wonder when this happened?' or 'I wonder who invented that', or 'I wonder how you make such and such?' or 'I wonder what the origin of that word is' . . . and then just leave it hanging. It makes me wonder how much they actually wonder, when all they have to do is take their phone out of their pocket and look it up.

Then I know people at the other end of the spectrum, who will always search online for the answer to questions, because they genuinely want to know. I remember driving past an impressively long wall in the middle of the countryside with someone, who promptly took out her phone and investigated. It turned out to be the longest brick wall in England, belonging to a family estate with a fascinating history which kept us entertained for the next hour of the journey.

Of course you can't get your phone out and start searching in the middle of a formal meeting, or a wedding, or when you're already late leaving the house – although you could make a mental note to look later. But you learn so much by exploring the internet, and it introduces you to things you'd never even thought about before. You wouldn't remember every single fact if you were tested on it a month later, but that doesn't matter. Some things will stick, and some will just leave you with a sense of a particular time or historical figure or event or way of thinking.

The search for knowledge is only one part of being curious, but it's an important part. And finding yourself wondering about a certain thing is a great place to start. You so often find, if you're of an inquisitive bent, that the thing you started out looking for is just a springboard into other things you never even knew about, and it's easy to spend a fascinating hour or so satisfying your curiosity about things you never knew you were curious about until you started looking.

Of course it doesn't have to be the internet. You might have books you can look things up in, or a friend you can ask, or you might just experiment – 'I wonder what a Marmite and mayo sandwich would taste like' or 'I wonder what happens if you put your whites and coloured clothes in the wash at the same time?' You might not like the answer, and you might wish you'd looked it up instead of trying it, but at least you'll know for next time. So when you catch yourself wondering, follow it up and find the answer. Otherwise you're not really wondering at all, are you?

> **YOU WOULDN'T REMEMBER EVERY SINGLE FACT IF YOU WERE TESTED ON IT A MONTH LATER, BUT THAT DOESN'T MATTER**

RULE 88

Expand

The last Rule was about continually searching for knowledge for the fun of it, in an ad hoc fashion. But you can also expand your mind in a more deliberate, intentional way. It's always good to keep learning because it means you keep broadening your perspective, your mind stays active and agile, it's fun and enriching to do something new that you enjoy, and it makes you a more interesting and rounded person too.

As we get old, it's easy to settle back into our comfort zone, but not only is this a waste of all the fun and stimulation we might otherwise have, there's research to show that keeping our curiosity alive can help stave off the kind of mental decline that often comes with age. So no skipping this Rule just because you're older and think you don't need it.

Do you remember sitting in lessons at school that you found really boring, and nothing seemed to go in? That's partly because if we're not interested, it's much harder to take in information. On the other hand, when we're really curious, the information just lands. So if you pick an area of learning, or a skill, that you're keen to learn, you'll find it much easier than you found Geography at school (for me it was definitely Geography).

There are so many different things you can set out to explore, from creative practices to psychology, practical skills to a period of history, scientific understanding to philosophy. You don't have to restrict yourself to one at a time, either. You could enrol on a course, or just read a book, join a book group or take an evening class. Come on, what have you always wished you could learn to do, or wanted to know more about?

You can pick an approach too, whether that's hands on, or getting a friend to teach you one-to-one, or being part of a group, or a class, or going on a retreat of some kind. You can expand existing skills, or start something new from scratch. Who knows where it will lead? That's half the fun. Your woodworking class could turn into a business, your reading around Shakespeare's life could become a fascination with sixteenth-century Europe. Or you might scratch that itch quite quickly and move on. It's all fine, because it's about giving yourself free rein to find out what intrigues you and then explore it.

It's good to give yourself variety too. If you're fascinated by history there are loads of books that will feed your interest, both factual and fictional, but don't always turn to a book. Next time pay a visit to an interesting site, or go to a museum, just mix it up a bit, because that will stimulate different parts of your mind. Otherwise it's like endlessly watching gardening programmes on TV without ever actually smelling a rose. It's giving you something, but it's not the full experience.

> **IT MAKES YOU A MORE INTERESTING AND ROUNDED PERSON**

RULE 89

Question your work

If curiosity benefits you in life generally, it should be no surprise that it is good for you at work along with everywhere else. People who are curious at work – and academically – are typically higher achievers, given that the more you want to learn, the more you will know. And the even better news is that those people who explore and question more at work report greater job satisfaction, as well as less stress, burnout, depression.

I've already talked about how bringing a curious mindset can benefit your relationships, both in general and specifically where there's any kind of conflict. This applies to work relationships as much as personal ones, and strong, positive work relationships go a long way to feeling happy at work, and to feeling supported when your workload is challenging.

But apart from your relationships with your colleagues, what exactly does it mean, being curious about your work? For a start, it means asking questions. Don't take anything for granted but always try to find out why we do things this way, what would happen if we changed this, why do we offer six colourways and not three or eight or ten, is there a way to speed up deliveries, why do we need to hold this meeting . . . you might ask these questions out loud, or you might explore them in your own mind.

On top of this, learn everything you can about the organisation and the sector you're in. Read, learn, get all the training you can. Try out ideas, and always be on the lookout for ways to do things better – cheaper, faster, higher quality. Talk to your colleagues about how you can make their lives easier, or whether you could work more productively if you pooled resources here, or allocated tasks differently there. You're a Rules Player, so you'll make sure you don't wind people up by seeming to know best or always telling them how to do their jobs.

You should be able to see that this kind of curiosity is the perfect starting point for being creative, and for problem solving, which are enjoyable, stimulating and valued traits to have at work. In other words, this approach will make your job more interesting, and will be appreciated by the boss.

Of course some companies encourage this kind of mindset more than others. If you're in a position of authority, you can encourage it in your team. Hopefully if your boss sees the benefits, they'll want you to develop it further. If you're stuck in one of those companies where they really don't want you to think for yourself, well, maybe you're not in the best job you could be. Rules Players need to be where they can shine.

> **THIS APPROACH WILL MAKE YOUR JOB MORE INTERESTING, AND WILL BE APPRECIATED BY THE BOSS**

RULE 90

Reject boredom

If you really embrace curiosity, one of the great advantages is that you never need to be bored again. There's always something to explore or learn or wonder about. Even when you're stuck in a waiting room or a queue or a long coach journey, you can entertain yourself amply just by seeing what you can learn.

One of your absolute go-to resources should be reading. Whether it's a book or a device or a website, reading is one of the best ways you can stimulate your curiosity. Read what you enjoy, it doesn't matter whether it's fiction or biography or history or travel or reference, it will all give you new information or new perspectives. Always aim to have some kind of reading material with you if there's the slightest chance you'll otherwise be bored. Why wouldn't you?

But of course, occasionally you'll be caught unawares by boredom, and you won't have anything to read. What then? One option is to look around you and spot things you wouldn't normally see – then consider what they tell you. For example, what does the dentist's waiting room tell you about the dentist? What sort of pictures have they chosen to hang on the walls, how much care have they taken to relax you, or entertain you?* Look at the people around you – what can you tell about them from the way they dress, behave, interact – or otherwise?

You might have an ongoing question to wrangle with in your mind. I have a friend who directs theatre shows, and occupies any free time with wondering how to stage her upcoming productions. She says there's always an effect or a mood that she feels she could achieve better, so thinking through possibilities and considering affordable solutions always passes the time when she has nothing else to do. In your case it might be designing your garden or picking the cricket team or restoring your classic car – there will

---

* Obviously not enough on this occasion

always be options you haven't considered, so now's your chance to think out what they might be.

Or you can simply pose yourself an interesting question and then try to arrive at an answer. I remember a conversation once, that lasted at least an hour, simply because someone said, 'Centaurs are interesting. They're the only animal I can think of – albeit mythical – that has two rib cages.' This led to wondering whether any other animal fitted this description (none that we could think of) and then speculating about which ribcage the heart would belong in (where's the most efficient place to pump from?) and whether the front legs would connect with shoulder or hip joints (no idea, but it makes a difference). It was a slightly bonkers conversation on account of centaurs being mythical so there was no way to check our conclusions, but it was much more interesting than playing I-spy.

> **THERE'S ALWAYS SOMETHING TO EXPLORE OR LEARN OR WONDER ABOUT**

SOUL

It's not easy to define your soul, and we wouldn't all express it the same way, but it has something to do with our human spirit that has nothing to do with physical or material things. If you follow a religion, organised or otherwise, you may well see it as that part of you that connects with some higher consciousness, and which perhaps outlives us.

Even if we struggle to define it, though, most of us understand that we have a spiritual aspect, whether we're Muslim, Christian, Hindu, Jewish, Buddhist, pagan or indeed humanist, or belong to any other religion or belief system. And when we connect with that part of us, we rise above short term and material concerns, and see the bigger picture.

This perspective is enormously helpful in coping with the day to day, and recognising that the little frustrations and upsets and conflicts will pass. So it's hardly surprising that the more time we spend consciously in that spiritual mindset, the less the little stuff will matter, and the happier we'll be. That's not to say that it's practical to live permanently in that state, unless you're a monk or a hermit, but you want to be able to drop into it easily when everyday life is getting on top of you.

There's pretty irrefutable research to show that people who regularly attend religious services – of any faith – report higher levels of happiness. However my observation is that people with a strong sense of soul benefit even without being part of an organised group – whether their own beliefs are individual, or whether they are part of an organised religion but don't fit attendance into their lives regularly. Whatever you believe, finding time to connect with your own soul will bring you peace, meaning, and a lasting sense of happiness.

RULE 91

Find a purpose

One of the most consistent research findings around happiness is that having a sense of purpose will increase your satisfaction with life. In other words, feeling that your life has meaning. That doesn't have to be the big stuff – contributing to world peace, solving global warming – it can be on as small a scale as you like, so long as it gives you a reason to get out of bed.

Your purpose might be to care for your kids, or to do everything you can to make your colleagues' lives as easy as possible, or to work in a job that benefits people in some way – which might be supporting them directly, or might be making a product that brings them joy or solves a problem. It might be to keep your local neighbourhood watch running smoothly, or to help clean up the local beach or park. It can be big or small, it doesn't matter, because it's not an objective measure. It's about the sense it gives you that your life has a value of some kind, to someone or something.

When you feel a sense of purpose it gives you a more positive outlook on life. You feel less anxious and more relaxed, less sad and more joyful. You'll also notice, from almost all the examples I've given you, that it generally involves other people – directly or indirectly – so it also fosters your sense of connection, and helps you to feel part of a community. Even if you don't regularly meet with that community, you know you belong to it.

Most of us live a life with some kind of purpose, but we don't always recognise it. If you don't have that sense that your life is meaningful, you need to find it. Think about who or what would lose out if you weren't here – your family, your clients, your colleagues, your environment, your club, your local group. Who values you? What do you contribute? What do you do that matters to you?

Once you think it through, you should be able to see that you have a role, a function, a purpose. Of course, when you think about it, you might also feel that you'd like it to be stronger. Perhaps you're passionate about the environment, but have such a busy life you don't do much about it beyond recycling your rubbish. In that case, think about how you can fit doing more into your life, so you feel you're making a valid contribution, however modest.

It's hard to overstate the importance of having a purpose in life, and recognising it. You will feel more connected to that bigger picture that nurturing your soul is all about, and that will bring you a sense of satisfaction that you'll never find in material things or transient experiences.

Be prepared for the fact that your purpose can change over time. When the kids leave home, when you change jobs, when you move to a new area, the things that give your life meaning may change. That's normal, and what matters is that you're aware of it and, if necessary, you find a new purpose.

> **IT CAN BE ON AS SMALL A SCALE AS YOU LIKE, SO LONG AS IT GIVES YOU A REASON TO GET OUT OF BED**

RULE 92

Live by your values

This follows on in many ways from the last Rule, although it's not the same thing. We all believe in certain things – whether we'd describe ourselves as religious or not – and we have our own moral compass. This will be personal to you, although it may have a lot in common with other people, especially those you spend a lot of time with. Most of us, for example, would believe that you shouldn't steal. Then again, some people would take that to mean that you shouldn't travel on public transport without paying, while others don't see anything wrong in that.

So your values won't be identical to everyone else's, even if they're similar. And what matters is that you live by your own values. If you don't believe it's right to get away without buying a bus ticket, you shouldn't do it. It's really important to be true to yourself, because the alternative is to let yourself down, to feel like a bit of a fraud, not to be able to sleep nights. It taints your soul, even just a little bit.

The bus ticket might not seem like a big deal, but it's the thin end of the wedge. Either you live by your values or you don't. Suppose you believe in helping other people, and then you're not there for your friend when they ask because you're busy at work and feeling tired. What if you believe in treating everyone with respect, and you're out with a group of friends who make racist or homophobic comments and you don't call them out? Perhaps you believe that people shouldn't be exploited, but you buy your clothes from cheap brands which exploit workers in developing countries.

See, it's not always easy to live up to your own standards, and they don't always coincide with other people's. Living by what you believe in sounds pretty easy until you think about it. Sometimes it is easy, but when it isn't you can't shirk it. Not if you want to feel clean and not be ashamed of yourself somewhere deep inside.

A strong spiritual life is important to your happiness, and that's much harder to achieve if you're a hypocrite on some level.

It's worth mentioning here that this isn't about imposing your values on other people. Within reason – and within the law – they're allowed to have different values from you. The aim isn't to convert them to your view, any more than you want them to pressure you into fare-dodging. Of course there's a point where you might question why you're hanging out with people who, to use the earlier example, are racist or homophobic, and that might be a very good question. However, there are lots of other issues where your friends' values are slightly different from your own and that shouldn't be a problem, so long as you both respect each other's beliefs. If you like a drink of an evening and your friend follows a faith that prohibits alcohol, you don't pressure them to drink. The same goes for the rest of their values that don't impact on you.

> **SOMETIMES IT IS EASY, BUT WHEN IT ISN'T YOU CAN'T SHIRK IT**

RULE 93

Find the awe

If your soul is that part of you that has nothing to do with the material world, surely the best way to connect with it is when you're physically separated from that world – when you're away from the trappings of wealth and stuff and materialism, and they're not pulling your focus in any way.

You must have had that experience of sitting on the cliffs overlooking a crashing sea, or being out in a thunderstorm, or standing at the top of a mountain, or in the silence of a deep forest, and feeling that, in the best way, you just don't matter. You're so tiny in relation to the wonder and vastness of what's around you, that your own problems seem insignificant. These things will still be here generations after you're gone, and that's reassuring and calming and liberating and wonderful.

Wonderful in the sense that it inspires wonder.* And it gives you that sense of connection to a bigger picture that puts your life in perspective and feeds your soul. This is something we need to do as often as possible, not just once in a blue moon, perhaps when we're on holiday. One of my very favourite places in the world is the foot of Skógafoss waterfall in Iceland, which I've been lucky enough to visit a couple of times, where the water thunders down in front of you, filling your vision and your ears and all your senses so that nothing else exists.

I can't get to Iceland very often unfortunately, so I have to be able to replicate this closer to home if I want to keep that connection fresh and regular and alive. We all do. Sometimes you're lucky enough to witness a powerful thunderstorm, or to travel past an

---

* I had an English teacher at school who wouldn't allow us to use any descriptive word unless we meant it literally. If we said something was awful he'd insist we justify precisely how it filled us with awe. I knew this was nonsense if only because he himself was clearly awful, despite singularly failing to fill me with awe

inspiring view. But you need to be able to find this feeling on a daily, or at least weekly, basis without relying on luck.

I know one person who likes to have an open fire in their house not just for warmth, or to feel cosy, but because they get this same sense when they stare into the flames. Another friend plants their garden for wildlife and can lose themselves for hours watching the butterflies, or following the route the bees take from flower to flower. You can live in the middle of a busy city and still find a way to connect with the awe-inspiring power of nature, and forget about your own troubles. So no excuses. Build it into your regular routine, even if it's only for a few minutes. It's always magical, and on a tough day it's about the most restorative thing you can do.

> **ON A TOUGH DAY IT'S ABOUT THE MOST RESTORATIVE THING YOU CAN DO**

RULE 94

Have a ritual

There's a reason why almost all religions have rituals. Humans have a deep need for ritual. It provides stability, reduces anxiety, offers a moment to focus on the spiritual, and is a way to mark the passage of time. There's evidence of human ritual practices going back tens of thousands of years, predating any of the official religions we recognise today.

Of course it's not only religions that use ritual. Sportspeople, for example, often have rituals they use before competing, which have been shown to reduce anxiety. In fact, the anxiety-suppressing benefits of this kind of ritual have been demonstrated in many studies, whether people are preparing for an exam, a performance, an interview, a talk or anything else.

If you follow an established religion you may already have your own rituals that you can apply to any situation, whether that involves taking part in a ceremony with other people, or just offering up a quick silent prayer. If you don't have such a structure to follow – or the one you have doesn't cover all eventualities for you – there's no reason you can't design your own. After all, every accepted ritual was made up originally, or has evolved through experiment, and a well-designed ritual will give you that same sense of stability, calm, spirituality, whether it comes from you or from anywhere else.

So what goes into a good ritual? It needs to be something you can do readily. If you use props – candles, incense, music, objects of significance – you might want a simplified version (or a different ritual) for those times you need to calm yourself before a performance or exam or difficult conversation. Next, you need to be able to forget everyday life while doing it, and focus on that spiritual connection, so probably don't design it for a busy family kitchen, for example. Pick somewhere quiet, indoors or outdoors, that you have easy access to. Don't create a 45-minute ritual unless you have time for it regularly. There's nothing wrong with a two- or three-minute routine, so long as it works for you.

Those are the practical considerations. As for the ritual itself, it should consist of a series of actions that you do in a fixed order, in a formal fashion. These behaviours should hold some kind of symbolic meaning for you. Not necessarily every single one – you might start with a ritualised process to put you in the right frame of mind, such as breathing exercises – but the overall ritual should symbolise something spiritual.

Now put together something that fits these guidelines, and that you can do as often as you like. Aim for at least a couple of times a week, ideally at a regular time, such as when you wake up, when you get home from work, just before bed. Have fun putting together something calming and meaningful, which becomes a habit.

Some people find ritual really beneficial and develop several practices throughout their day. For example a brief moment of thankfulness every time you make a cup of tea – like a secular take on saying grace – or a moment to open the window and breathe in the night air. If it's formalised, consistent, and symbolic of something spiritual, it's a ritual.

> **THERE'S A REASON WHY ALMOST ALL RELIGIONS HAVE RITUALS**

RULE 95

Stop trying to find yourself

I've lived in Glastonbury, so I know about people trying to 'find themselves'. I've done it myself, in the distant past. But it's not only fruitless, it's counterproductive. I'm not talking about understanding yourself, which is something we should all try to do. The more of a grasp you have on why you think, feel and behave the way you do, the better chance you have of modifying the things that aren't working for you. Easing the bad feelings, curbing the unhelpful behaviour.

These things are the result of nurture, or nature, or your life experiences, and the better you understand them, the easier it becomes to build your self-esteem and to feel in control of your life and your actions. You can interpret the phrase 'finding yourself' in lots of ways, and if this is what you mean by it, then carry on.

However if you mean trying to find some kind of spiritual awakening by looking inside yourself, enlightenment through introspection, forget it. That's antithetical to the whole concept of soul, which is about connecting to something outside yourself. Something that is much bigger than you, and puts you and your worries into perspective. It's not about navel-gazing.

I've known people try to find themselves because life has damaged them and they're looking for some kind of healing, and I can entirely sympathise with that. However, beyond understanding themselves a bit better, I've rarely seen any of these people become happier for it. I've known many others who have clearly enjoyed the process because it makes the whole exercise all about them, and they're the kind of people who like things to be all about them. It never makes them into better, or happier, people though.

The thing that's worth searching for is the bigger connection that works for you. Something to believe in. If you're lucky, you'll already know what that is. You might belong to a recognised faith, or have found one that feels right. Or you might be agnostic or atheist, in which case it can help to find something else that gives you that bigger picture in a way that you can relate to and feel comfortable with.

More and more people without a recognised faith, an organised religion, are turning to beliefs such as humanism or paganism, because these give them a perspective on their own lives, and something to focus on that is outside themselves and still feeds their souls. So if you don't find it in you to be Christian, Muslim, Jewish, Sikh or any other atheistic religion, you can still find something to believe in.

> **IT'S NOT ABOUT NAVEL-GAZING**

RULE 96

What goes around, comes around

There's something very clean and refreshing about doing something for nothing. It gives you a good feeling to be so selfless, and if you can incorporate it into your life as an abiding principle, it does your soul good. It's simply a matter of defaulting at helping people when you can, without looking for any return or recompense from them. Looking after your neighbour's pet when they're away, sitting all evening with your friend because they're upset, lending a bit of money to your brother when they're in a bit of a mess, giving up your time to help with a local cause.

This is all about being a part of the bigger picture, the wider community, and developing a sense that we're all in this together and we put in what we can. You'll get the most out of this approach if you don't look for any reward but, of course, if you're part of that community, sooner or later you'll be on the receiving end yourself.

The idea of paying it forward is that when you do something for the next person, instead of repaying the favour to you, they do it for someone else. That person then pays it onwards again, and so it goes. Sooner or later the universe will repay you, whether with the same favour or a different one. Benjamin Franklin once famously lent another man money, with the stipulation that rather than repay him, this man do the same thing for someone else, with the same condition, and so on. That way, he said, it would be possible to do a lot of good with only a little money.

If you have the money, that's a great way to use it. But if you don't have that kind of money, it works just as well with any other kind of support and help. You may or may not want to make the stipulation – in an ideal world you shouldn't have to, because everyone will take it as read.

When you're the one who needs support, and the people around you help out, there's no need to feel guilty or indebted. Sooner or later you *will* get back what you put in, even if it's not in quite the same format. If everyone's in it together, then everyone who gives to you has received from somewhere, and it all goes round in a big happy circle. Your supporter today might not be the same person whose dog you looked after last weekend, but that doesn't matter. Just like a co-operative, everyone puts in what they can, and everyone takes out what they need.

So make this a Rule to live by and yes, a few people will want to take and not give, but they'll be a small minority. Meantime you'll be able to feel good about yourself, feed your soul, and accept what comes back to you with appreciation and no sense of obligation.

> **EVERYONE PUTS IN WHAT THEY CAN, AND EVERYONE TAKES OUT WHAT THEY NEED**

RULE 97

Think about what comes next

You can't think about your soul – that immortal part of you, separate from your physical, material being – without thinking about what happens to it when you die. If you don't already have a strong belief around this, you need to consider it. You're not going to find irrefutable proof, but you at least need to arrive at a best guess. You can't simply ignore the question.

Why not? Because you can't possibly know how to live this life if you have no idea where it fits into the grand scheme. Are you living your only life? Is this one of many? Is there an afterlife of some kind? The answer – your best answer – to this question has to affect what drives you.

There are many structured belief systems which hold that you move on to some kind of heaven or nirvana or enlightenment. Others believe that you return, perhaps many times, maybe until you get it right. And others that would say this is it. When you die, that's that. End of.

So are you living this life in order to earn your way to a blessed afterlife, a heavenly paradise, where you'll face some kind of judgement when you die to determine if you've passed the test or not? If so, that's going to come with a pretty clear set of rules you need to live by in order to make the grade. Or will you be coming back in some form, in which case you may be able to determine what kind of life form you reappear as? Again, you'll want to pay attention to the rules if you care whether you're a worm or a whale or a pet dog. Or are the sins of this life going to be revisited on you karmically? You might come back as a human, but the advantages – or disadvantages – you'll be born with will be established according to how virtuous you've been this time around, how much positive karma you've banked.

And if you think that death is the end, that still doesn't let you off the hook. If this one life is all you have, what's the point of it? What can you do with it that makes sense? Eat, drink and be merry? Make it one big party, because this is your only chance? Or maybe use it to do everything possible to make the world a better place for the people who come after you?

Whatever you believe about death will inform how you live your life, so you need to know what it is that you do believe, or you'll ultimately be rudderless. One of my beliefs is that the love you have for other people outlives you, whether or not your consciousness does. I get a warm feeling from being loved by people who happen to be out of the room for the moment, and I can feel that continuing even when they're permanently absent. At low times, I can be sustained by the love I know someone felt for me when they were alive. So one of my drivers is to do whatever I can to ensure that the people I love will still feel the warmth of my love and support when I'm gone.

> **YOU'RE NOT GOING TO FIND IRREFUTABLE PROOF, BUT YOU AT LEAST NEED TO ARRIVE AT A BEST GUESS**

RULE 98

Don't ask 'why me?'

Life throws all kinds of things in your way, and there's no such thing as a life without hardship of some kind. Of course some of us are luckier than others, but no one gets through unscathed. And although you wouldn't ask for any of the bad things that happen to you, actually a seamless easy path through life would be pretty uninspiring. You'd learn nothing about yourself, you'd have little in common with the rest of humanity, and how could you really appreciate the highs if there aren't any lows?

Nevertheless, it's easy to find yourself asking 'why me?' when the next buffet hits. What did you do to deserve this? Some people find themselves questioning whether it's somehow their own fault that everything seems to get dumped on them. Of course sometimes people bring specific things on themselves, but in terms of life in general, I can tell you that it's not your fault, and there isn't a reason why it happens to you.

Obviously that might seem scary. If you have no control, you can't stop it happening. Well yes, that's true, but on the other hand it means it's not your responsibility, not your fault. That's quite liberating actually. All you have to do is learn to roll with the punches.

And if you're not in charge, who is? That's the big question. Many religions have an answer to that, whether it's god, destiny, kismet, fate. Maybe it's just chance. I dunno, who do you reckon is up there pulling all the strings? Or do you think there's just a tangled mess and no one is even trying to sort it out?

Whoever is in charge, it certainly isn't you, or me. Sometimes I think they're doing OK all things considered, and sometimes I think they're doing a rubbish job, whoever they are. Still, I couldn't do any better. And I wouldn't want the responsibility either. Ah, there's the thing again that always reassures me – at least I'm not answerable for the whims of the universe.

I'm not expected to know what's round the corner, it's not my fault when everything gets knocked for six, whatever's going to happen isn't my problem. Above my pay grade. All I have to do is accept it. There's some higher authority making all the rules, and I just have to take what I'm given. It's a bit like being a small child, or being at school. You're told here's your ration, this is your test result, take your hat off indoors, don't speak until you're spoken to. Frustrating on the one hand, but also much easier than trying to make up your own ground rules. Leave all that to the universe, or whoever is calling the shots. We still have some obligations – it's up to us how we react, how we behave, in response to this random stuff being thrown at us. But all we really have to do is sit back and wait for the next thing. Who knows, the next thing might be wonderful! Meanwhile, no guilt, no blame, no questioning ourselves.

> **IT'S NOT YOUR FAULT,
> AND THERE ISN'T A REASON
> WHY IT HAPPENS TO YOU**

RULE 99

Not all questions have answers

I find modern science endlessly intriguing and rewarding, giving us the answers to so many things we've never understood before, and opening up more questions which will no doubt be answered eventually. There was a time when people believed that the Sun went round the Earth, or that base metal could be transmuted into gold. Increasingly we're moving towards a point where we have at least some idea about the things we don't yet know for certain, where we can disprove certain explanations even if we can't yet categorically establish the true one.

Nevertheless, there are some things that science will never explain because they defy scientific analysis. There are those who like to pooh pooh anything that can't be scientifically demonstrated, but absence of proof is not the same thing as proof of absence. In other words, just because you can't prove it, doesn't mean it *might* not be true.

There is room in the world for magic and wonder and mystery, and if you want to nurture your soul, you'll find space for it in yourself too. As Hamlet said, 'There are more things in heaven and earth than are dreamt of in your philosophy'.* And that's a good thing, because if everything could be reduced to quantum physics and string theory, fascinating though they are, the world would be a less extraordinary, incredible, magical place.

So don't dismiss things as bunkum just because they don't seem plausible to you. I'd be the first to acknowledge – having lived in Glastonbury, as I've mentioned – that there is any amount of wibbly, New Age, hippie twaddle out there. Of course the vast

---

* I'm allowed to (mis)quote Shakespeare too, because he died over 400 years ago

majority of it doesn't stand up to serious scrutiny, but it's human nature for many people to believe what they want to believe.

In among all the pseudoscience and hokum, however, there are just occasionally things that really do defy explanation. Or at least scientific explanation. And too many people are inclined to say they can't be true because there's no rational way to account for them. That if they can't be real on a scientific level, they can't be real on any level.

But there are other levels, other planes – maybe not physical ones – where the extraordinary can be true. And if you refuse to accept that, you are reducing your existence to a very soulless one. It becomes very hard to believe in anything, when faith has to be replaced by hard knowledge, and that impoverishes all of us. So if you want to enrich your soul, set aside at least a little space for magic, for mystery, and for questions that have no answer.

> **THERE ARE SOME THINGS THAT SCIENCE WILL NEVER EXPLAIN BECAUSE THEY DEFY SCIENTIFIC ANALYSIS**

RULE 100

Get better and better

One of the most valuable aspects of developing your spiritual life is that it's really impossible to do it without improving yourself in the process. And by feeling that you're a better, more rounded person, you feed your soul. So it's a virtuous circle.

In order to find a conscious purpose in life, to be true to your own values, to pay it forward, you have to really think about who you are and what you're for, how you live and what you want. It's quite possible simply to understand yourself, warts and all, and to accept yourself with all your faults and vices. That's fair enough – we're all human and we shouldn't set unattainable targets for ourselves or we'll just keep feeling we've failed.

However once you listen to your soul, you realise that while you shouldn't expect perfection, that doesn't mean you can't aim for it. You can travel that road without any expectation of arriving, but with a determination to keep moving forwards.

Many of the Rules for the soul – and indeed other Rules too – require you to understand yourself better. You need to be conscious about your actions, your feelings, your thoughts, your beliefs. You need to question yourself, and get to know yourself in ways you may not have done before.

And once you really start to know yourself, what motivates you, what influences you, what made you the way you are, it's difficult not to see ways in which you can improve yourself. You begin to understand the unhelpful patterns you sometimes follow, or why you struggle with certain situations, or are prone to particular difficult feelings. Once you see it, it often doesn't take much to see what changes, tweaks, new habits, will help to make your life easier, and to make you into a better, more productive, happier, more valuable, more content version of yourself.

We all deserve to be as happy as possible. Not to chase after fleeting moments of excitement or elation or thrills, lovely as they can be, but to focus our attention on pursuing the more lasting kinds of happiness – satisfaction, contentment, a sense of being comfortable in our own skin. Looking after your soul means nurturing the bigger picture, and looking after those big, overarching things that really matter in life. The things that will stay with you, and sustain you, permanently.

> **WE ALL DESERVE TO BE AS HAPPY AS POSSIBLE**

Create your own Rules

Remember, I'm not the only one who can observe other people and see what works for them that could work for me too. So keep a look out for new Rules, and when you identify one I haven't included here, note it down. Keep a list of additional Rules you want to emulate and write them down. You can share them too so we all benefit.

If you're wondering what makes a good Rule, it's a guiding principle that works in (almost) all cases for people of all kinds. It's not just a handy trick or a useful tip (e.g. use coloured stickers to organise yourself, or keep your car de-icer in the house and not the car – you always need it when you're at home anyway, and that way the bottle isn't freezing cold – or never eat anything bigger than your head). Useful as these pointers are, they're not Rules in the sense I use the word. A good Rule is about changing your attitude or shifting your mindset so you approach problems or situations from a different perspective.

It seems a shame to keep these new Rules to yourself, so please feel free to share them with other people. If you'd like to share them on my Facebook page I'd love to hear from you at www.facebook.com/richardtemplar. Either post a single Rule, or maybe put together your top five and post them so other readers can get the benefit.

When you decide to share a Rule, it's a good idea to explain it, and then to give an example or two so other people can see how it works in practice, to help them understand how to apply it to their own lives.

A Rule is a Rule, it doesn't matter whether it's me or you or anyone else who has noted it down (in fact, it doesn't matter if no one has identified it yet, it's still a Rule). If it works, not only for you but for other people too, it's worth sharing. So please post your new Rules and, who knows, I may even assemble the best of them together sometime in the future.

Index

achievement 32–3
adventure 190–1
advice
  asking for 88–9
  taking 80–1
alcohol 170–1
assertiveness 4, 7
awe 206–7

blame, accepting 54–5
boredom 198–9
brain
  creativity and 25, 42–3
  sleep and 158
brainstorming 28–9
breaks, taking 162–3
breathing exercises 96–7

capabilities, confidence
  and 8–9
charities 76–7
choices
  character and 62
  confidence and 8, 9
  health and 157, 158, 173
  making 23
  responsibility for 50, 58–9
  time and 118
coffee 171
collaboration, creativity
  and 38–9
comfort zone 12, 179,
  191, 194

commitment 51
  making 18–19
communities 154–5, 218
comparisons, avoiding 14–15
complaining 48–9, 124
compliments 84, 85, 86
confidence
  avoiding comparisons 14–15
  benefits from 3
  capabilities 8–9
  commitment, making 18–19
  decision-making 22–3
  facing up to fears 20–1
  negativity, avoiding 10–11
  personal strengths and 4–5
  self-belief and 16–17
  taking time 12–13
  value and 6–7
conflict 186–7
connection, social 135
  balance in 142–3
  community and 154–5
  developing 144–5
  distractions and 140–1
  friendships, work 152–3
  improving 144–5
  quality of relationships
    136–7, 142
  social activities 150–1
  with strangers 148–9
  time spent on 138–9
  viewpoint, other 146–7

control
  over actions 47, 55, 56–7
  of life 52, 58
coping strategies 132
creativity 25
  achievement 32–3
  brain and 42–3
  collaboration 38–9
  flow 26–7
  inspiration 40–1
  mistakes and 30–1
  negativity, avoiding 28–9
  problem solving 25, 29, 34–5
  rule breaking 44–5
  self-expression 36–7
criticism
  constructive 29, 62, 63
  by others 10, 11
  self-criticism 110, 182
curiosity 179
  adventure and 190–1
  boredom and 198–9
  conflict and 186–7
  expanding skills 194–5
  learning journey and 180–1
  looking for interesting information 188–9
  about people 184–5
  questions 182–3
  satisfying 192–3
  about work 196–7

death 214–15
decision making 67
  confidence and 3, 22–3
detachment 99, 101, 102, 104–5

diet 168–9
distractions, social connection and 140–1
Donne, John 37
dopamine 40, 179, 180

emotions
  feeling 110–11
  unwanted 110–11
empathy 54, 83, 146, 147, 187
energy
  levels 177
  managing 166–7
expertise, recognition of 8–9
exploitation 51–2

faith 211
family 4, 11, 73, 78, 138, 141
fears, overcoming 20–1
feedback 89
  welcoming 62–3
  avoiding 10–11
finding yourself' 210–11
flow 26–7
Franklin, Benjamin 212
focus, failure of 100–1
fresh air 160–1
friends
  deep 184
  developing 144–5
  intrusive 82–3
  negative feedback and 10
  superficial 144, 145
  supportive 72, 82
  time with 141
  values of 205
  at work 152–3

giving 69
  accepting and 86–7
  advice and 80–1
  charities 76–7
  forms of 70–1
  indebtedness and 78–9
  by others 88–9
  and receiving 72–3
  small acts of 74–5
  thanks 84–5, 86
  unwanted help 82–3
habits 23, 114, 168, 220
happy place 122–3
health
  breaks, taking 162–3
  choices, making 172–3, 175
  diet 168–9
  drinking 170–1
  energy levels 166–7
  exercise 164–5
  fresh air 160–1
  immunity 174–5
  long-term 176–7
  sleep 158–9
honesty 11
Howe, Elias 34

immune system 174–5
indebtedness 78–9
inquisitiveness *see* curiosity
insomnia 95, 158–9
inspiration 40–1
irritability 6

Jarman, Derek 40
job satisfaction 196–7
judgement 106–7

learning 198–9
likeability 6–7
liquid intake 170–1
loneliness 135

mindfulness
  basics of 95–6
  breathing exercises 96–7
  definition 91
  detachment 104–5
  emotions, feeling 110–11
  focus, failure of 100–1
  observation 98–9, 103–4
  opening up 106–7
  values, retention of 108–9
  Western form of 93–4
mistakes
  admitting 52–3, 55, 61
  learning from 30–1
mobile phones 130–1
Monet, Claude 45
money 3
mood
  creativity and 25
  detachment and 101
  fresh air and 160
  health and 176, 177
  judgement and 106
  relationships and 136
negativity, avoiding
  confidence and 10–11
  creativity and 28–9

pets 142–3
poverty 135
power 3
praise 84, 85, 86, 87

prescription drugs 172
problem solving 25, 29, 34–5
purpose, finding 202–3
questions
  conflict and 186–7
  personal 184–5

random acts of kindness 74
reading 198
reassurance 22
recreational drugs 172
relationships, close 136–7
  see also family; friends
relaxation 124–5
religion 201
responsibility 46
  blame, taking 54–5
  for choices 50, 58–9
  control over reactions 56–7
  exploitation, avoid 51–2
  feedback, welcoming 62–3
  mistakes, admitting 52–3
  for others 60–1
  social conscience 66–7
  for team 64–5
  victim, avoid being 48–9, 50
  for yourself 58–9
risk-taking 3
ritual 208–9
routine 114, 115
rule breaking 44–5

science 216–17
self-assurance 12
self-belief, confidence and 16–17, 19
self-esteem 3, 10

advice, refusing, and 82
creativity and 34, 36
giving and 69
self-expression 36–7, 40
self-identity 37
self understanding 182–3
Shakespeare, William 44–5
skills 4
  sharing 71
sleep 158–9
smoking 172–3
social activities 150–1
social anxiety 3, 4
social conscience 66–7
social relationships *see* connection, social
soul *see* spirituality
spirituality 201
  awe 206–7
  death 214–15
  developing 220–1
  doing favours 212–13
  fault and 216–17
  'finding youself' 210–11
  purpose, finding 202–3
  ritual 208–9
  science and 218–19
  values, living by 204–5
standards, high 128–9
strangers, talking to 148–9
strengths, personal 4–5
stress 56–7, 124
  immune system and 175
  mistakes and 52–3
  standards and 128–9
success 3

Tennyson, Alfred, Lord 181
thanks, giving 84–5, 86
time 113
   chores 114–15, 116–17
   happiness and 122–3
   how to spend 118–19
   overfilling diary 124–5
   phones and 130–1
   postponing activities and 132–3
   priorities and 126–7
   social relationships and 138–9
   standards and 128–9
   taking 12–13
   work/life balance 120–1
tobacco 172
trust in yourself 5
values 6–7
   confidence and 6–7
   living by 204–5
   personal 6–7
   retention of 108–9
vapes 172
victim, avoid being 48–9, 50, 51
vulnerability, showing 145
water consumption 170–1, 172, 175
wealth 14, 135, 206
work/life balance 120–1